*Leisure:
Perspectives
on Education
and Policy*

Leisure: Perspectives on Education and Policy

by
Max Kaplan

National Education Association
Washington, D.C.

Stock No. 1495-2-00 (paper)
          1494-4-00 (cloth)

Note:
The opinions expressed in this publication should not be construed as representing the policy or position of the National Education Association. Materials published as part of the NEA *Aspects of Learning Series* are intended to be discussion documents for teachers who are concerned with specialized interests of the profession.

Library of Congress Cataloging in Publication Data

Kaplan, Max
    Leisure.

    (Aspects of learning)
    Includes bibliographical references.
    1. Leisure—Social aspects. 2. Leisure—Social aspects—United States. 3. Leisure—Study and teaching—United States. 4. United States—Social conditions—1960-   I. Title. II. Series.
GV14.45.K36   790'.0135   77-28598
ISBN 0-8106-1495-2
ISBN 0-8106-1494-4 pbk.

For Barbara

—M. K.

The Author

Dr. Max Kaplan is Director of the Leisure Studies Program, University of South Florida, Tampa.

Books on Leisure

By Max Kaplan

Educational and Leisure-Time Activities of the Elderly, with C. Attias-Donfut. Prague: European Centre for Leisure and Education, 1973.

Leisure in America: A Social Inquiry. New York: John Wiley and Sons, 1960. Paperback edition, 1965.

Leisure, Lifestyle and Lifespan: Directions for Gerontology. Philadelphia: W. B. Saunders Company, 1978.

Leisure: Theory and Policy. New York: John Wiley and Sons, 1975.

Technology, Human Values and Leisure, with Phillip Bosserman. Nashville: Abingdon Press, 1972.

The Consultants

The following educators reviewed the manuscript and provided helpful comments and suggestions: John Arch, Elementary School Teacher, Park Avenue Public School, Nashville, Tennessee; Dr. Nelson Butler, Department of Leisure Studies, Salisbury State College, Salisbury, Maryland; and Janet Permuy, Physical Education Teacher, Shorecrest Preparatory School, St. Petersburg, Florida.

Contents

Preface

The subject of leisure, it would seem, can hardly be discussed in any depth without touching on education. Skills are obtained as children that eventually affect such leisure forms as physical activity, sociability, mind-life, aesthetic sensitivity, civic commitments, and use of the mass media. No serious analysis of leisure—however its parameters are drawn—can ignore the matter of values, goals, lifestyles, or what I have elsewhere called the "mastery of self." Only a superficial view of leisure identifies it through activities, or evaluates it by standards of the "fun morality."

As one of the essays in this volume notes, while relaxation or withdrawal from work is an essential element of leisure, the most intensive and serious commitments can also be the leisure of some persons, as in composition of a poem, solution of a scientific problem, or voluntary service in a hospital.

European education, while not ignoring the skills to maintain the society, has emphasized the goal of personal enrichment. It is no accident that many delegates to the United Nations from those nations are Ph.Ds; a broad education fits one for public service. By contrast, courses in the humanities and social sciences among many American universities in the 1970s had to be justified as relevant—not to the good life, but to "marketable" usefulness for careers. Some of our students must have been puzzled or amused when their French counterparts went on a nationwide strike in 1976 against the move by government to overhaul French higher education in the direction of more job skills.

Even before Sputnik, the emphasis in all levels of education in the United States has been toward preparation for making a living, in spite of lip service to broader goals. Much of the criticism of our education is that it does not prepare students to "cope" in banks and stores; or they cannot name their Senators or fix light fuses. As a consequence, the arts are often the first to be eliminated from the curriculum in times of financial stress; yet, as the Harris poll of 1976 clearly indicates, the American population now recognizes the importance of the arts to a degree far beyond the situation of several decades ago, and is willing to pay for it. The arts may be "extracurricular" in the schools; they have become increasingly essential in the home and the community.

Again, it is no accident that every country in eastern and western Europe (Japan can be added since 1972) maintains major research programs on leisure, in an attempt to balance social and technological change with the preservation of its traditional cultural values. Among such university, academy, and ministry programs are those in Sussex, Paris, Lund, Prague, Moscow, Budapest, Brussels, Hamburg, Utrecht, Warsaw, and Waterloo and Trois Rivieres in Canada. In the United States, some universities are reaching out from recreation toward comprehensive leisure studies; only one, the University of South Florida, undertook a full commitment as early as 1967; one other, Salisbury State College in Maryland, has offered a BA degree in leisure studies since 1977. In Indiana, there is presently a demonstration program, LEAP, funded to the National Recreation and Park Association by the Lilly Endowment, Inc. "to develop a model curriculum in leisure education for the public school system."

This volume, then, is based on the assumption that to supplement, perhaps to reinforce, such programs as LEAP in the schools, there is need for a broad introduction to substantive issues that enter into "leisure studies." Sufficient footnotes are provided to assist those who wish to pursue the matter in greater depth or range. One caveat is necessary here: There is as yet no consensus among leisure scholars and observers in the United States or internationally as to methodology, issues, or even the meaning of "leisure." However, those who expect more of this young field are respectfully invited to find more than minimal consensus in such established fields as philosophy, economics, or sociology . . . . My 1975 volume, *Leisure: Theory and Policy,* quoted within the body of this work, presents the most complete statement among my own writings; to some extent as an indication of growth within the field as a whole, it invites a comparison of data and references to my volume of 1960, *Leisure in America: A Social Inquiry.*

The essays presented here, even those that have appeared elsewhere, have been updated or modified. Their origin is noted below:

Chapter 1. Origins of the new leisure: four mini-revolutions. First publication.

Chapter 2. New concepts of leisure today. *Leisure Today: Selected Readings.* Washington, D.C.: American Association for Leisure and Recreation, 1975.

Chapter 3. Leisure education—for whom, with whom, by whom? *Proceedings of the Third National Leisure Education Conference,* Indiana University Department of Recreation and Park Administration in cooperation with the Society of Park and Recreation Educator Branch of the National Recreation and Park Association, January 16-18, 1977, Indiana University.

Chapter 4. A new language for a new leisure. Originally presented to the Southern Association of Departments of English, February 11,

1972. Published *Bulletin of the Association of Departments of English*. New York City; No. 33, May 1972.

Chapter 5. Personal tensions, leisure, and futurology. Prepared for the Conference on Futures Research, IRADES, Rome, September 1973.

Chapter 6. The arts and recreation. Unpublished; prepared as working paper for planning committee conferences on arts and recreation, 1973, co-sponsored by National Park and Recreation Association, the U.S. Park Service, and the National Endowment for the Arts.

Chapter 7. Leisure, human values, and religion. Prepared for a conference on this title, co-sponsored by the University of Minnesota Department of Physical Education and Recreation and the Leisure Education Resource Center of the National Lutheran Campus Ministry, April 1976.

Chapter 8. The urban framework for new work and leisure. Unpublished; read to Deutsche Gesselschaft fur Friezeit Conference to Commemorate the 600th Anniversary of Krefeld, Republic of Germany, September 4, 1973.

Chapter 9. The implications of leisure theory for gerontology. Presented to the IIIrd International Course of Social Gerontology, Dubrovnik, Yugoslavia, May 15–19, 1972. *Leisure and the 3rd Age*. Paris: International Center of Social Gerontology, 1972.

Chapter 10. Leisure and the design profession. American Iron and Steel Institute, March 23, 1972; published by the Institute as *Lifestyle 2000: Designing for the Third Millenium*, 1972.

Chapter 11. Business, labor, and the four-day work week. Unpublished.

Chapter 12. Leisure and the general process of theory/policy. Unpublished.

Leisure:
Perspectives
on Education
and Policy

CHAPTER 1

Origins of
the New Leisure:
Four Mini-Revolutions

Four sources of the new leisure may be alliterated—*social morphology, cybernetic maximization, 60-minute magnification,* and *St. Peter-esque mobility.* Altogether, they constitute a new framework for the national direction. Each in itself points to a new reality—indeed, a mini-revolution which sets the background for the new characteristics of leisure and its implications.

The demographer Philip Hauser introduced the term "social morphology" to denote population *explosion* or dramatic growth, population *implosion* in the form of urban concentration, and population *diversification* or the in-gathering of heterogeneous backgrounds and tastes. As he noted, "The social morphological revolution is closely interrelated with other revolutions—agricultural, commercial, scientific, technological and industrial."[1]

As to population explosion, it took humans two billion years to reach a population of one billion—not until 1830. Each succeeding billion took only a fraction of this time: the second only 100 years later, 1930; the third in 30 years, 1960; the fourth, fifth, and sixth billions in population will come in 13, then 11, then 9 years, reaching the six-billion mark by 1995. By 1973, the world's population had reached 3.7 billion.

If leisure for the mass has developed primarily in the industrialized, urbanized centers, and in the more economically abundant societies, then what has happened demographically after the Industrial Revolution is highly relevant to our subject. How did the growing population fare economically and where did it go? The facts show, indeed, that two types of populations arose, divided substantially into the worlds of the rich and the poor, literate and illiterate, urban and rural, overfed and underweight,

15

consumption-oriented and survival-oriented. By 1850, the ratio between incomes in these two constellations was 2 to 1; in 1950, the disparity approached 10 to 1; by 1960, 15 to 1. In 1970, the per capita income in the United States was $4,100; in India, $90. By the year 2000, this difference may grow as 50 to 1, or $10,000 as against $215.

Obviously, urban growth or population implosion has been dramatic. At the time of our first census in 1790, 95 percent of all Americans lived in rural areas; even by 1900 we had only four cities with populations of one million, comprising 17 percent of the total population. To take one example within this large picture, the black segment of the population has been affected deeply by its change from 73 percent rural to 73 percent urban by the last half of the century.

Diversification within the urban population has served as the rationale for specialization within the leisure framework and, of course, has enhanced the urban or metropolitan community, attracting immigrants from the small towns and rural areas.

Much can be said of the industrial and technological bases of today's leisure. Wilensky has noted that previous societies have taken more days off from work than our own.[2] However, they were holy days. Automation and computerization are qualitatively different from former industrial changes, and over a period of decades, they have cast serious doubt on the view of classical economics that employment will not be affected. What they have done is to bring about the transition from manufacturing and agricultural jobs to a large service sector that now comprises six of every ten workers. Even though we have seen only the beginning of computerization, by 1970, already one million Americans were employed in some aspect of this business. The number of programmers grew from 100,000 to 175,000 during the four years before 1970. From 1955 to 1970, the total number of computers in the United States shot up from 200 to 85,000. By 1980, their number will probably reach 210,000. Internationally proportionally larger growth took place between 1960 and 1968: While the number of computers increased by 14 times here, it increased by 28 times in Europe and by 100 times in Japan.

The progressive economist Robert Theobald may overstate in his view that in a decade we can expect that tens of millions will be unemployed, on public welfare, or on public works programs; but Robert Davis, formerly the principal scientist for the Systems Development Corporation, foresees that component cybernation in industry will be the rule rather than the exception, enabling plants to foresee product demand; control inventories of raw materials; produce, inspect, and store finished items; and bill customers, all coordinated by a single computer. The computer industry, already the fastest growing industry, will in a few decades become the world's largest industry.

Can anyone deny the potential choices that this, among other technological and managerial developments, will open to management and workers at a time when American labor unions encourage this change in energy if negotiations protect their members? In Europe I have long been impressed by the direct participation of such unions as the English Trades Union Congress in its members' leisure-time life—such as adult education—a dimension of time for which they take some justified credit. Our own unions, with notable exceptions (the garment workers and electrical workers in New York) have shown less participation. Donald Michael foresees:

> . . . a nation with a large portion of its people doing, directly or indirectly, the endless public tasks that the welfare state needs and that the government will allow to be cybernated because of the serious unemployment that would result. These people will work shorter hours, with much time for the pursuit of leisure activities.

Sixty-minute magnification is the third mini-revolution of our time. In 1900 the hour had the same astronomical 60 minutes as today, but then it provided less access to distances, to friends, to images of the world, or to anything else that has extended our reach into places and experiences. Inflation makes the dollar less useful, and the hour is affected, as there are less dollars to buy transportation, communications, or other tools of leisure. But practically all Americans already had a television set by the mid-70's, and over 67.1 percent had a color television set in 1974. As to cars, it is only calculated mythology that they should be changed every few years; inflation does not deny the consumer a car as much as it undercuts the Madison Avenue and Main Street hawkers. It is worth emphasizing that our new measure of wealth is *access*, not dollars; enlarged alternatives in the free hours provide one new form of access. The old *dollar* could buy more than today's dollar; but the new *hour* offers greater potential than the old as a content for experiences, and it exists in a freer psycho-sociological and institutional context.

The hour may also be enlarged in its potential in terms of its relation to other free hours. Sunday night may have a different connotation if I don't go to work on Monday. The thousands of hours in one's retirement, say from 60 to 75, are unlike any other hours during the so-called "productive" years. Also, three days of free time are potentially different from three days spread through the month—more bulk or bloc time to be bored, or more bulk time to permit a fishing trip. The "value" of the four-day work week or the flexitime patterns now coming into western Europe (by which the industrial or office worker—like professors—has more choice in her/his work and leisure rhythms) leaves the purely economic consideration of productivity and moves into the realms of psychological perception, social aspirations, and philosophical values.

Finally, a new interest in leisure has resulted from what may be profanely called an "urban renewal in heaven." Heaven has been not only improved, but also relocated. Improvement came by taking away all waiting and even much praying; it has become instant, simply by way of the credit card. Why wait—and work hard in those years of waiting—for some unknown cosmic ethereal existence when Pan Am will provide real and immediate comforts as you wing around the world in *80 payments?* Leisure has not only effected a material heaven, but has also relocated it *within* familiar regions—in one's home, in one's neighborhood, in the football stadium, the bingo hall, all around the church (but not *in* it). Heaven takes on many forms, and the degree of abundance, regardless of inflation, has brought enough books, records, concerts, gadgets, tools, boats, camping equipment, and sports spectacles to accommodate all candidates, whether sinners or saints. Leisure for the common person of all classes and tastes has not killed God, as the old preachers warned; it has made every one of us a goddess or god.

These, then, are four mini-revolutions: in population, mechanization, enlarged alternatives through new time resources, and fulfillment of new aspirations during one's lifetime. If they are carefully re-read, an important observation emerges: All of these changes go beyond America. They pertain to all countries where industrialization takes hold. The internationalism of industrialization also transforms the nature of issues that emerge. The issues of yesterday, relating to a few cases such as England and the United States, were dealt with brilliantly by Veblen (revised in an updated but also outdated way by Lindner) and revolved around *social class;* as we approach the "post-industrial" societies today the issue of leisure (as Ellul and Toraine spell it out correctly) is related to the meaning of technology for all classes. This is an issue that confronts Asia and eastern and western Europe. Indeed, in 1973, we held a significant conference with UNESCO on "Cultural Innovation in Technological and Post-Industrial Societies"; and according to Dr. R. Bammate, former director of UNESCO's Division for Social Studies, this eight-year study program which is now under way in the United States was initially proposed by a bloc of the underdeveloped nations! Their concern was with the impact of technology on their cultural values.

If, then, leisure has become an issue of worldwide proportions, it is well to review briefly in the next chapter some new concepts of leisure, primarily to open our minds to its growing dimensions.

CHAPTER 2

New Concepts
of Leisure
Today

How does one interpret the impressions of recent travels far into eastern Europe; the visual scenes—endless sheep being led up to the mountains of Yugoslavia, the picturesque *dorfs* of Romania, the Kesckemet market near Budapest, or the teeming bazaars of Sarajevo, Skopie, and Istanbul; the aural contrasts on the car radio of modern symphonic sounds a tiny millimeter away from endless folksongs, the intellectual exchanges of unguarded home conversations, and the more formal interviews with cautious academic and political figures?

In Bucharest, the head of research for Romanian television, discussing political controls over mass media, insisted that TV has a life of its own, but that in contrast to McLuhan's "world village," his listeners are joining the "world metropolis." Television is only 11 years old in Romania, and already one of every 28—half a million people—has a set; the favorite programs are on science, followed by melodrama shows. He used this contrast to say that social change is therefore inevitable, not only in industrial and institutional life, but in values as well.

This duality in change came out of all the conversations, and with it, a hunger for scientific studies from the United States, where the change in lifestyles through industrialization has been longer under way. Hungary is just now becoming a consumer-oriented society; Yugoslavia, longer experienced in the determination of its economic policies, is now anxious for American studies on aging. But throughout western Europe as well, in studies of leisure which go to the heart of national directions, we find this pairing of issues: (1) a growing accessibility to more goods, services, and knowledge; (2) an implicit question of changing values, traditions, and attitudes, not only among the young but also among all ages. East and west, there is a concern with the future, not only in a general sense, but also in systematic study, with leisure as one overall clue to what people will need and want beyond maintenance. They see in leisure a summation of an indicator of aspirations as well as an adaptation of the new and the old, one affecting the other.

This research goes on everywhere, in universities, in academies of science, or, as in Bucharest, in the research unit on social aspects of medicine which is now seeking to conceptualize the relationships among emotional, mental, and biological health. The University of Zagreb has a large department for studies of leisure within its Institute for Social Research; it has completed studies on retired persons (especially those formerly active in sports) and has made community studies of Zagreb and 74 small towns and on the nature of youth clubs, family life, and leisure patterns at the university itself.

The Government Survey Service of England has published a national study of outdoor recreation. Major studies of sample populations across the USSR have been aimed at reducing commuting time and household work. The group in Paris, headed by Joffre Dumazedier, the foremost authority in our field, not only heads a seven-nation team but also has carried out intensive inventories, as well as theoretical tasks, in the town of Annecy and elsewhere. Similar work is being done in Holland, Denmark, Italy, and elsewhere.

But the question is not to catalog but to interpret this growing body of independent and comparative study. The tendencies which I see are toward a new view of leisure as (1) holistic in its conception and function, (2) dynamic and developmental in its methods, and (3) futuristic and policy-oriented in its intent.

A *holistic approach*, rather than a segmentalist approach, embraces the two formerly opposed conceptions of leisure: as ends or as means. The first was derived from Greek aristocrats who, living off slavery, could afford to meet in their academies to speak eloquently of grand themes such as justice or beauty, to participate—as "volunteers," we would say—in the political process, or to enjoy the great plays and sports events. This is the use of nonwork time in developing the mind, the conscience, and the good life. Sebastian de Grazia in *Of Time, Work and Leisure* brings this notion up to date in brilliant fashion—the notion of *pa̓idaia*: leisure as an end, as contemplation, joy, scholarship, as something beyond the material base or value.[1] The Catholic philosopher Joseph Pieper sought in *Leisure, the Basis of Culture* to revive this pro-Protestant ethic and to stress leisure as celebration of life.[2]

The second view, grounded in the ethic of work and post-Hellenic Christianity, is to look upon leisure as therapy, rest, relaxation, social control, re-creation for subsequent productive effort—and generally, therefore, as instrumental in character. Identified with the needs of the workers of history, the last century has also seen this approach broadened into the dimension of leisure as a symbol of the rich, most notably in Veblen's work[3]; as a tool for status by all; and, most specifically, as part of the personality configuration in David Riesman's work.[4]

We seem to have attributed the so-called Puritan ethic to the laboring classes, not the rich. We have forgotten how difficult is was in the early decades of the English industrial revolution to get people adapted to factory schedules, and we have seen how quickly the common people get used to such comparative luxuries as the two-day weekend. While in Czechoslovakia I was told that their Russian "guardians" have been unable to get the workers back to a six-day week after the Czechs had been enjoying a five-day week the one year before 1968.

The whole subject, therefore, was approached almost to the middle of this century in either a general, philosophical, moralistic tone on the one hand, or with a suspicion of mass culture by the intellectuals on the other hand. It was not surprising, therefore, that when social scientists took up the subject of nonwork (an inescapable inquiry in observing social change), they reacted by detailed studies of consumer expenditures, time uses, class distinctions, and the like. There were often correlations, as evidenced by Havighurst's studies of activities with factor analysis,[5] Wilensky's work on the leisure of various types of "organization men,"[6] or the work of the Lazarsfeld group on uses of mass media.[7]

The current holistic tendency, when one looks at the balance of European as well as American research, seems to blend these two traditions—leisure as an end and as a means of relaxation and revitalization. An attempt at this synthesis comes, interestingly, from the Russians, who do not speak openly now of leisure as time for potential service to the socialist society, but of personality growth. However, they hang onto the "parks for culture" tradition by their own interpretation of personality, as in this statement from three members in the Siberian Department of the USSR Academy of Science:

> In the capitalist society, rest and entertainment are held as most valuable; they are connected, first of all, with consumption of goods and services and take people away from the sphere where a highly developed personality can express itself [politics, arts, technological activity].[8]

In the western countries, too, we seem to be looking for a conception broad enough to include both views, not because a scientific theory would be easier, but because we are interested now in leisure as a social phenomenon. Objective data, correlations, hypotheses, experiments, and other tools of hard science remain useful to this larger conceptualization, but the newer task demands more. As Dumazedier notes, the subject is now too large for merely a quantitative elaboration of such categories as play, sports, arts, social life, etc.

> Seen in the complex of its multiple relations to other aspects of our mechanized and democratic civilization, leisure is no longer a minor item, postscript to the major ones, to be studied or not, depending on whether there is time or money left. . . . Leisure is, on the contrary, the very central element in the life culture of millions upon millions of workers. It has a deep-going, intricate relatedness to the largest questions of work, family, and politics, and these, therefore, must now be reexamined and reformulated.[9]

In this light my own conceptualization is that leisure is not an activity, but a construct of elements which are emphasized with roles that are pertinent to the construct rather than to economic, political, educative, religious, or marital life. These elements may, in modified form, be found in other institutions as well. Leisure, then, can be said to consist of *relatively self-determined activities and experiences that fall into one's economically free-time roles, that are seen as leisure by participants, that are psychologically pleasant in anticipation and recollection, that potentially cover the whole range of commitment and intensity, that contain characteristic norms and restraints, and that provide opportunities for recreation, personal growth, and service to others.*

This conception, it seems to me as I work out the implications of every phrase, permits both traditions to be observed in union and separately (leisure as manifestation of our desire to be human—our "essence"—and of our desire to develop symbols and tools in the mastery of ourselves and our environment—humans as "history").

I have talked at some length of the holistic approach to leisure. More briefly, I turn to its new *dynamic and developmental approach.* Riesman's *The Lonely Crowd* illustrates one such example. Thrasher's old gang studies, Becker's work on marijuana, Lynd's observations in Muncie, deJager's research of symphony audiences in Utrecht, chapters by Margaret Mead and others in volume 22 among reports of the Outdoor Recreation Resources Review Commission—all these and others are not snapshot or static views of leisure; they seek to examine processes, dynamics, developments. Every form of data is useful.[10] For example, there now exists an enormous collection of time-budget studies, covering 12 nations (including the United States), engineered by a genius at such cross-cultural endeavors, Alexander Szalai of Budapest, formerly deputy chief of research training for UNITAR. This is the most successful cross-cultural study that has ever been done; two volumes on the uses of time summarize and interpret the data of 130,000 cards and 50,000 interviews. They tell us much about how people in Jackson, Michigan; Gyor, Hungary; and other communities spent a specific 1,440 minutes of their lives in the middle 1960's. Such data *per se* are useful as a beginning. We now know, for example, that in the socialist countries, men spend 7% of their leisure in study and self-education, while only 2.3% do so in capitalist countries; that, except for the use of mass media, remarkably comparable periods emerge in both cultures for such items as social activity, sports, entertainment, rest, reading, and talking.[11]

However, a dynamic view would have to place such data against each milieu in a complex of explanatory factors. The Szalai group does some of this, of course, but within the material it has uncovered. Many questions can be raised, combining humanistic with scientific inquiry. A male subject reports, truthfully, that he attended an opera yesterday; what is unreported, and crucial to his life meaning, is why he went, how often he has gone before, and what it has meant for his aesthetic sensitivity, whether he intends to go again, whom he met, what he eliminated from his normal routine, and so on. Thus, longitudinal studies are one corrective, despite the difficulty of eliminating the intervening variables.

Recently, some of my college students carried out family interviews on leisure. They began with the resources of the community and neighborhood; observed the outside of the home; inventoried relevant objects inside; obtained basic data about the family; asked about individual, subgroup, and joint activity; and then turned from a tentative conclusion about the dynamics of *this* family to a hypothesis about families with similar characteristics. Or, starting from an activity as such (listening to a lecture or drinking beer), we interrelate four components—objective conditions, selection, use, and meaning—as the first level of explanation; this is placed within a level of related pairs (person–family, group–subculture, community–region, nation–world); all this falls within the cultural pattern (systems of energy, social organization, values, and symbols); finally a classification of social orders completes the whole, proceeding not by historical periods, but by types of structures which I privately call Conquest, Kilowatt, Cogno, and Cultivated social orders. Thus, we have moved, in an accumulation of complexity, from the fact that someone who does not have to is at this moment listening to a dull lecture, all the way to the type of utopia she/he conceives or at least implies in her/his symbolic leisure selection.

This study of large configurations is interdisciplinary. It draws from history, economics, psychology, sociology, linguistics, anthropology, philosophy, and common sense. I see this dynamic approach developing in the gerontologists' use of the term "aging" rather than "aged." Criminology has long ago left a static explanation or treatment—at least in the books—as have family work, services to the handicapped children, and other fields.

Students of leisure can contribute by interpreting nonwork as diagnostic or explanatory clues for lifestyle. The social sciences can contribute to the leisure student by noting characteristic behavior in various social situations that help us to understand the milieu behind leisure uses. Urban planners, for example, are coming to the position that cities are more than storehouses for goods and services; they are also scenes of drama, human aspirations and relationships, and living tradition.

Thus, leisure is now seen as both holistic and dynamic. A third new conception is its relation to *futurism and policy.*

The futurology movement—we think of such men as Buckminster Fuller in Illinois, Bertrand deJouvenal in Paris, Herman Kahn on the Hudson, Robert Jungk in Vienna—has had to look at time as a new basic resource. Ozbekan of the Rand Corporation has spelled out to this new discipline the sticky problem of assessing or projecting changing values.[12].

For the traditional social scientist, futurology is a new discipline which succeeds or fails on its careful projections. However, the scientific heretic seeks not to eschew her/his tradition but to synthetize her/his knowledge with the pragmatic policy-making segment of society; the future is in some part a matter of our making. As U Thant has said, yesterday we used to assess our resources and set our goals; today we can establish priorities and create the necessary resources. Look, for example, at only a few striking elements that enter the future in relation to leisure:

1. American business and industry seem to awaken to the worker's right to distribute her/his time in accord with her/his rhythm of life. Thus, there arises a significant difference between her/his use of what I call "bulk" time in contrast to "fragmentary" time. So-called practical persons who rule business are naively surprised that many workers prefer to work 40 hours per week, but within four days. Yet how long should it take personnel managers to discover that a person will be more productive, loyal, and happy if she/he has some choice and flexibility in the distribution of work and nonwork hours? A concentrated 13-week paid sabbatical among steel workers is far different from a distribution of 58 off-days over a longer period of time.

2. Without analysis, I submit the increasing uselessness of all comparative data that are based on hours or on income and that are more than a quarter century old because an hour is not an astronomical unit of time but, socially, an interval which provides opportunities, and these possibilities (as in travel and communications) keep going up as the value of the dollar keeps going down.

3. There is a new fusion—I call it the "neo-primitive" aspect of the post-industrial society—between day and night, far and near, young and old, male and female, domestic and international, inside and outside, urban and rural, work and retirement, labor and leisure. Even our familiar indexes of poverty are to me increasingly useless if we go beyond hunger

itself and deal with access, not only to food and shelter, but also to literacy, distance, friendships, and to the world itself.

4. There emerges a new flexibility in lifestyles: the prospect of the four-hour day for the many, of retirement at 38 by 2000 A.D., or of normal and healthy life to the ages of 90 and 95 projected by Alex Comfort and other gerontologists. This suggests that the old sequential pattern of social roles may be radically shaken. The worker may prefer to work all day one week and not at all next week, or—as Juanita Kreps suggests—half a year, or half a lifetime.[13]

Our field might, if these broad propositions hold up under careful analysis, contribute enormously in conceptualizing some bold outlines for this flexibility-time life. Can scenarios—in Herman Kahn's language—be created to envision family life where the father works half a year?[14] Can adult educators conceive new roles to serve a potential ongoing clientele of many more millions? Can government units on all levels, together with private service agencies, invent new leisure occupations, as Dennis Gabor suggests in his important volume *Inventing the Future*?[15] Can the current effort contribute vision, courage, and innovation to develop a unified national program for volunteerism?

These policies cannot, in our society, be as unified as in the socialist nations. But even there, as I was told in each country, "we want to know what you are doing, but we must develop the Romanian way in our politics and our traditions." So, too, in the United States. Our post-industrial material base is available, in spite of sizeable poverty. But even poverty has different origins and meanings in every culture; so, I would add, does abundance. The question that looms before us all is not the distribution of our trillion-dollar gross national product. That we can do if we wish it. What we have not achieved in a mature fashion is a theoretical frame for the study of leisure of our time, or a philosophical position on values for its application in the emerging social order.

As to those values, the most important clue is what youth is saying, not in a systematic way, but in the setting aside of material goals—indeed, even the artifacts themselves. The questions they ask are familiar ones, but they come from a generation already raised, as far as they are concerned, in the post-industrial society where physicists are moralists, old political processes do not respond to change rapidly enough, education prepares them to produce what can better be made by machines, adults become neurotic over such playful symbols as long hair, and their nation has sent them to die in a costly war which they see as immoral, useless, and founded on an historical fraud. These are children of leisure who are by now experts at organization and at tweedling even the federal bureaucracy by gestures of opposition and affirmation, whether in Estes Park or Washington.

These, then, are several new undercurrents that I see in our field— holism, dynamism, futurism. As we collectively face the problem of constructing a thesaurus for computerizing the flood of data, we must realize our internal differences and theoretical gropings. But each of us needs to stand up, state her/his piece, and know when to sit.

This is our problem: to relate the older tradition and the newer tradition of humans with the help of such miracles as electronics, computers, and Boeing 747's. But let us not confuse the trip itself with the substance of the old or the new. As Thoreau said it, let those in the technological society not become the tool of their tools. Leisure is both a tool and an end. What we do now with our time will be entered into the passport to the future. As Eric Hoffer reminds us, let us make sure we do not forget that passport. To enrich the leisure of today will be to arrive at our goals tomorrow, and to deserve to travel into the future.

CHAPTER 3

Leisure Education— for Whom, with Whom, by Whom?

When an editor recently invited me to read a manuscript on theories of play, he commented that the recreation/leisure field seems to be amorphous, uncertain of its directions. His perspective, of course, was influenced by a concern with the potential sale of books. But can those of us in the leisure field not all agree, from our perspective of the profession itself?

One is aware of national and international agencies that speak for the leisure profession: AAHPER (American Alliance for Health, Physical Education, and Recreation), NRPA (National Recreation and Park Association), ELRA (European Leisure and Recreation Association), WLRA (World Leisure and Recreation Association), SPREE (the research commission within the International Sociological Association), the Van Cle Foundation of Antwerp, and others that are being formed. On the one hand, there is cause to celebrate this proliferation in organization, research, education, and, perhaps, influence. On the other hand, the overlapping of purposes or the jockeying for power is a reflection, in part, of gaps in communication, of the youthful vitality of our movement, and of a problem in identifying our goals. A quarter of a century ago, when my interest in this field of study became serious, I had difficulty in finding respectable material for my first volume; my recent manuscript, on the other hand, had to be cut in half to form a readable work, for the problem by then was the plethora of materials. Nowadays no one can keep up with the literature, especially if the international scene is her/his panorama.

There are immediate reasons for the worldwide interest in leisure and recreation with the coming of intensive industrialization. Underdeveloped nations are asking, or are being asked by such agencies as the World Bank, what the impact of new highways, tourism, television, and computers will be on their cultural heritage. A bloc of such nations asked UNESCO to engage in an eight-year study of cultural innovation in the United States, and later in other western and Asian areas, to observe the destiny of creativity and of leisure in technological and post-industrial societies.

The middle-range nations have similarly become aware of leisure as a clue to the balance between technology and tradition. Iran is a case in point. For its current five-year program, the Shah and his planners have committed themselves to a balance between material building through their oil wealth and preservation of their old Islamic traditions. My last trip there was to help their thinking about a new university which, as a contribution toward balance, will be devoted entirely to the old and the contemporary arts.

On a personal, daily level of existence, workers in all countries are not conscious of such national policies; they have been working hard, and seek every chance now to enlarge the time they may get for more fishing, reading, loafing, drinking, or any of the many other activities revealed in the 12-nation study carried on by Alexander Szalai and his colleages in the eastern and western European nations and the United States.[1] For example, during my 1974 visit to Warsaw, the main topic of policy and research concern—whether in the University, in the Polish Academy of Sciences, or within the various political ministries—was the probable impact of the imminent change from six to twelve free Saturdays during the coming year for all workers! This will be examined further in Chapter 12.

In the more advanced western nations, a collective concern with social directions is evident in a Council of Europe study of 14 towns in almost as many countries.[2] Intending to confine these inquiries to the state of the arts, the investigators realized that this could best be done through a more comprehensive study of leisure as a whole, for one issue is the division of time between the various forms of interest. For example, in Tempere, Finland, the fact that six of every ten adults had attended live theater during the prior year was traced to the cultural program initiated in the last century by labor unions as part of their conscious preparation for personal life in the forthcoming industrial expansion.

In the United States an additional reason that more leisure has become part of the new ethic is that our democratized, materially rich, and secularized leisure is profitable to many industries, from boat builders to the mass media.

But mainly, it is the change in everyday life that has created a need for the serious study of leisure and recreation. Many types of data are available to us. In terms of work hours we are down to about 2,000 per year, compared to 3,000 at the turn of the century; in terms of leisure expenditures, we are up to about 15% of the total consuming economy if we include transportation for pleasure; in terms of images, we have momentary access to all parts of the world through our mass media; in terms of daily habits, the average three-year-old has put in as many hours watching shows like *Sesame Street* as the students of Indiana University have sat before their teachers earning a B.A.; and the adult of 62 years will have spent a total of nine years in watching television on a time frame of 8 hours a day, 5 days a week; in terms of domestic change, the middle-class American has available every minute of the 1,440 in a 24-hour day appliances to heat, wash, cool, light, cook, clean, awaken, or entertain. In short, the material base for eliminating work and making life more comfortable that is now available to the average American is remarkably higher than it was for the Russian nobility of the last century whose magnificent costumes I saw at the Metropolitan Museum of Art. And just above this exhibit, the Egyptian display reminded me of the multitude of slaves who knew little else but work in those ancient days. Slavery to labor—actual or psychological—is less and less acceptable to the workers of our day, and the evidence seems to suggest that the goal of heaven, preached in a rough way throughout the past several thousand years by Christianity, is the essence of the so-called post-industrial society. It is a goal in which, as Aristotle saw, the looms will weave by themselves; in which individuals can enjoy health, travel, physical comforts, mental stimulation, creative expression, commitment to performing social services of their choice, and respect for what they have achieved in a long life. Indeed, without wishing to exaggerate either the prospect or the possibilities of the future, I have taken the public position that what we really mean by the "new leisure" is that by soft-pedalling the old work or Puritan ethic and accepting the new lifestyle of personal growth through the use of machines, we have transplanted heaven to earth; now, we need not pray that we will attain a Paradise through hard work; our new problem is whether, given the new choices during our lifetime, we can live with some degree of maturity, inner freedom, and choice, given our access to alternatives.[3]

This, then, is the issue for those in the profession of leisure and recreation: to serve as watchers and *animateurs* or leaders, so that the cosmic confrontation is more heaven than hell, more creative than distructive. The quest for direction, even the cry for help, is clear, for the new freedom is strange and often difficult, not only for Americans, but for those of other nations and cultures as well.

In spite of all this awareness and search for direction among nations, industries, and workers, the amorphous state of our profession that was noted by the editor may be due to our preoccupation with the minutiae of budgets, recalcitrant board members, intra-agency squabbles, and leaks in the park pool. I submit, therefore, that the profession must work to educate itself. Are we dealing sufficiently and in depth with implications of the post-industrial era? Do our students know Ellul, Dumazedier, Toraine, Szalai, Fuller, Fromm, Myrdaz, Kahn, de Jouvenal, the issues of *Society and Leisure*, or the important Czech Academy report on *Civilization at the Crossroads*? Can they and their faculties write with authority for *Business Week*, with lucidity for *Reader's Digest*, with depth for *Commentary*, with vision for *The Futurist*, or with practicality for *Family Circle*? Do we know enough, within the profession, about the 5,000 persons who turn 65 each day, with the view of understanding retirement as a form of leisure? Do we speak with conviction to bored employees, hesitant personnel managers, ulcerized executives, and skeptical labor leaders? Some years ago I consulted with CBS for their segment on leisure as part of a series called *21st Century*; I asked the obvious question: Why had they not, first of all, gone to the professionals? So little has the profession made its impact on decision makers for the masses.

The model for our internal communication and self-education might be the Tanglewood Symposium, a two-year experience of self-assessment by the Music Educators National Conference (MENC). Their membership was well over 50,000. Social changes had overtaken them as well by the mid-60s. Realizing the need to communicate with economists, philosophers, sociologists, business and labor leaders, mass media administrators, foundation heads, educators, and the clergy, the MENC allocated a modest sum to develop this dialogue. To help establish some consensus on its own philosophy, a working paper was prepared by Dr. Robert Choate and myself, containing succinct statements of social change in various areas, the kinds of questions that are relevant to the profession, and bibliographical suggestions. This document was printed for open reaction by the membership, and committees of informed leaders in each of eight regional districts were invited to engage in a close analysis and response to the document. Thus, eight critiques were available to the planning committee as it gathered outsiders to the site of Boston Symphony concerts in the summertime, for a full week of dialogue in plenary and group sessions. Aside from 15 nationally recognized music educators, the Tanglewood Symposium enjoyed an interchange with such persons as F.S.C. Northrop, the Yale philosopher; Max Lerner, the sociologist and journalist; Abram Maslow, the psychologist; such musicians as Stan Kenton and Gunther Schuller; a priest; a U.S. Steel Foundation executive; Olga Madar of the UAW; an official of the Public Broadcasting Corporation; the editor of a rock journal; and young students.

The final report was written by the several committees which included both "internal" and "invited" participants; it caught the flavor of plenary sessions; it reflected a new self-awareness among the so-called establishment of the music education profession. The report, now over a decade old, has had a decided, if immeasurable, impact on the profession.[4] Long, critical, and intensive preparation was the clue to this impact.

The MENC model needs to be modified for our present purposes in order to lay the groundwork for a national plan; my hope would be that the final plan would involve all the national professional leisure groups. The issues are far larger than those that presently, for historical or substantive reasons, fragment our efforts. Our themes or topics for extended discussion and dialogue would include, among others, trends toward further technology, the restructuring of work, an international professional structure, the mass media, and education throughout literature. Relating to an additional topic, our position as a profession in terms of the federal government is a major example of the interrelationship between our self-assessment and the larger society and its values. President Carter's commitment to reorganization, of course, has to go beyond lines of authority or management issues, into the substance of functions of departments and bureaus. A primary question for us, and for the government in its dialogue with us, is the degree to which the subject of leisure (however defined) becomes visible as a matter of public policy:

> . . . we have the right to ask whether the federal government is now equipped to deal with issues of leisure. The answer is clearly no. Nowhere is there an agency in which a total view can be obtained or on which holistic or integrated action can be taken. Bits of the picture are handled, in typical governmental structure, by innumerable agencies, such as offices of aging, education, commerce, or interior. On almost any issue, of course, there is some unavoidable, occasionally even desirable, overlapping; we would expect, for example, that the agencies concerned with parks will carry on special studies on travel patterns to national areas even though the Department of Commerce is simultaneously studying broad transportation and travel patterns. Yet, at a point in American history, each central interest has been given a centralizing agency for purposes of providing the main thrust for active functioning—labor, agriculture, business, education and the like.

The position is here taken that already, with 15 percent of our consuming expenditure devoted to "recreation," we are about ready for a central federal vehicle devoted to this interest; and this aspect of American life will inevitably grow more central. Such a vehicle could and, in the shuffling of bureaucracies, probably would be placed within an ongoing agency, such as HEW. My view is that this would be a mistake, assuring less attention than the times warrant. It is conceivable, but hardly probable, that the Department of Labor could be extended in name and purpose, "The Department of Labor and Leisure." More germane and effective would be a new commission comparable to the Atomic Energy Commission or the Civil Aeronautics Board in its independence to incorporate the general concern with future directions, but with dramatic pinpointing of new work issues of the post-industrial era; perhaps it could be called the Commission on Leisure and the Quality of Living.[5]

In succeeding paragraphs of the material quoted I suggest the responsibilities for such a commission in the areas of data collection, philosophy, implementations, and evaluation. In letters to President Carter, both before and after his election, I commented along these lines and proposed such a commission that would cross governmental and private agencies. Since both Vice President Mondale and Secretary Kreps have well-established reputations in the field of aging, I turn to this area as an example of one in which both the federal government and our profession will have a growing concern and in which numerous levels of interaction already exist through the Office of Aging within HEW; the Institute for Aging (hopefully with Dr. Robert Butler as its ongoing director); such national agencies as NCOA (National Council on Aging) and AARP (American Association of Retired Persons) and the National Association of Senior Centers; associations of nursing homes; and, most directly, the millions of older persons who come to our community centers or live in our communities.

Among the 28 millions over 60 will be found differences of intelligence, taste, and educational and occupational backgrounds comparable to those that characterize the younger generations. What is unique is not that 60 percent of the elderly are fully retired, or that a quarter of them are under the poverty line, or that 5 percent of them are in nursing homes, or that women outnumber men, or that they are living longer; all these facts are well known. We must counter what Butler has called "ageism," the prejudice and ignorance about the elderly that even many of the elderly have come to accept. The great task that the leisure profession confronts is to undo one of history's brutal conspiracies, robbing these people of ongoing usefulness to themselves and to the society.

No task exceeds this for our field, for at their simplest, our programs can keep older persons busy; little ingenuity is needed for that. Can we go further and help them to find new roles and responsibilities through leisure, to contribute to the community, to grow, to innovate, to preserve and enlarge their dignity and *menschlichkeit*?

One of our difficulties is philosophical for the keystone of much recreational programming is sheer activity *per se*, not role formation through activity. Another difficulty is the recreation profession's accent on *leadership*, which may be appropriate with children, rather than on *consultantship* and *colleagueship*, which are more appropriate with mature adults. A third problem, which goes back to the self-education I spoke of earlier, is our tendency to start with programs rather than with people. Another, of course, is that for historical reasons, the recreation movement has been identified with games, fun, sports, terminal goals, amusement, and play. We see evidence of such outdated thinking in Alex Comfort's *A Good Age* in his prescription, "What the retired need, what the unemployed need . . . isn't 'leisure,' it's occupation. . . . Get occupation, first. Leisure in the right sense will follow, if you have the time for it."[6] Those who know the contemporary thinking on leisure are aware of the broad approach which includes potential elements of creativity, serious commitment, personal growth, and service to others. Alex Comfort knows much about gerontology, biology, and sex, but little about the meanings of leisure.

In spite of these difficulties—conceptional, historical, and programmatic—we remain the clearest professional umbrella under which the elderly can find an ongoing use of their skills and experiences. Without appearing imperial, our concerns cover education, the arts, and civic action, as well as games, travel, entertainment, and sociability.

What we mean by the field of "leisure," as I view it, is an interdisciplinary discipline that extracts, synthesizes, and generalizes data or observations from all the sciences and humanities that have a bearing on the origins, structuring, uses, and perceptions of nonwork time; these generalizations are then available to such applied fields as education, urban planning, criminology, government, social welfare, the arts, the mass media, business, labor, gerontology, and recreation. Technically, then, if the study of leisure prepares us to unravel the elements of social change around the element of time, the study of recreation examines social structures or programs with the aim of bringing about more satisfying and creative use of such time.

The difference is that the education of a leisure professional is that of a historian, sociologist, psychologist, economist, philosopher, anthropologist, or generalist who attempts to utilize bits from all of them, depending on the issues one selects for study. Joffre Dumazedier comes out of French sociology, with a typical European dose of history and philosophy; Phillip Bosserman comes out of social ethics, influenced by the sociology of Gurevich; John Neulinger brings to leisure his psychological background; Sebastian de Grazia, political science, history, philosophy. The education of a recreationist is more concretely precribed, and increasingly draws from theoretical leisure studies as it continues to group work, community resources, park management, personnel management, public relations, and the like. As to public influence, leisure scholars probably have more impact on governments of western and eastern Europe than they do here. Perhaps the recreation wing of the profession in the United States has more power because of its decentralization on local and county levels.

The theorists and programmers find themselves on common ground in that, ultimately, science and policy (or R&D, as they say in industry) are interdependent. The public, and even the university community, is unaware or uninterested in these technical decisions.

Think of a tree, with its roots, trunk, and branches. The roots are all of the sciences and humanities; recreation is one of the branches, responsive to momentary conditions of the enviroment, but interrelated to all the other branches, such as adult education or tourism; in between is the trunk as a bridge, a connection within the full organism. We can, in an arbitrary but useful way, comment on some relations of these dimensions of the total tree to the areas I have discussed—self-education, government, and the elderly.

As to self-education, we can learn from the tree analogy that the *inherent* integrality is not enough; it must become *systematically* and *consciously* evident to each of the components: pure knowledge (the roots), generalization and social projection (the trunk), and delivery of services to the public (the branches). The wholeness also implies equality and interdependence, in contrast to the typical isolation and pecking order on the campus.

However, the communications must go deeper than the change of a departmental name from "recreation" to the new status term, "leisure." If some such plan is developed as described for the music educator, some difficulty will be encountered in communications. I remain convinced after 10 years of experience with it at the University of South Florida that an "institute" or "program" instrument is useful as a synthesizing unit. The Department of Leisure Studies at Salisbury State College in Maryland provides an interesting experiment with a degree-granting program that will subsume all three levels of the tree through its formal tie with at least 10 disciplines.

Yet, I submit a second major goal in our professional self-education is a frank recognition of our respective, specialized responsibilities. Reading the current literature of the recreation profession, where there is a serious attempt to touch on research, the tendency is to fall victim to quantitative studies without an awareness that in the social sciences *per se*, a disillusionment has set in with the purely empirical; the younger generation has been reading the old and the contemporary masters who could think as well as count—Weber, Ellul, and even Sorokin. My mentor, the Polish sociologist Florian Znaniecki, can be immensely helpful in this analysis of social roles, as in the study of the elderly.

I need hardly balance the picture by noting that leisure theorists are often unwilling or unable to visualize the bridge from their work to that of policy makers. Yet we should not be surprised at our respective parochialisms. A research mind and an administrative or programming mind move in different ways, and deal with characteristic traditions of thought and ultimate purposes.

As to government, if a special commission were to be established, it should expect from leisure theorists an ability to project new work patterns and probable impact on use of free time; or to help establish fruitful contact with philosophers and historians or goals for an emerging climate of life. From the recreation specialist, governmental programs will increasingly expect an ability to construct or to participate in networks of community services, such as are more prevalent in England than here, and described in

Leisure and the Family Life Cycle.[7] The day of isolated, single-purpose, single-generational services and financing will decline; as recreation planners are already aware, there are funds for recreation in agencies for family life, mental health, human relations, aging, the handicapped, and the arts.

As to the elderly, I have perhaps said enough. From the theorists we need more fundamental thinking on such issues as perceptions of time and the bridging from work to nonwork values; community recreation specialists have been unimaginative in developing programs that use the skills of the elderly; their ability to bring about creative mixing of the young and the old is presently at a primitive level.

I have used the elderly as an example of one segment to whom we can address our efforts, and from whom we can learn. There are also the business community, the labor community, the middle-aged women now finding their own lifestyles; there is a vast segment of public school administrators who need education on the implications of new time frames in the present and future lives of their students; there is the nervous mass media industry with its short-range goals and mythology of ratings, completely unconcerned with audience development. The problem is not that of identifying those who need us or those whom we need, but of becoming aware of the informational, perceptual, and power flows in our society, and making our priority efforts in those areas that will penetrate the farthest. The problem is one of recognizing other branches of the same tree.

The final issue is to see other trees in the forest of many interests that constitute life and culture. Can leisure, in its fullest sense, be studied or absorbed without a study of religion, economics, politics, and philosophy? There is a rational sense in perceiving or organizing this phenomenon we call "leisure"; there is equal sense in perceiving the whole panorama of human history and changes.

CHAPTER 4

A New Language for a New Leisure

For those of us from the field of leisure, it is entirely natural that those involved in the language and literature tradition seek to recognize the roots of their field in the interdisciplinary content. We are in part rooted in the Hellenic concept of *paidia,* or leisure as contemplation or love of life and thought and art; in contrast to this aristocratic, gentlemanly tradition, we are also steeped in the more democratic instrumentalist or therapeutic tradition—leisure as social control, mental health, self-expression, status, crime prevention, and family togetherness. Those in language and literature share the duality—language and literature as a form of beauty in itself and also as a means of communication.

But beyond analogies, there is a more substantive and crucial relationship between our fields. The great bulk of fiction—on the page, screen, or stage—has as its subject the depiction of human relationships and lifestyles which deals far more with the general areas of play, sex, friendship, conversation, fantasies, travel, aspirations, and momentary fragments of informal action than with expositions of work tasks. Much of the novelist's or dramatist's attention goes, therefore, to what might often be called leisure experiences, although little attention has been given to this common ground by scholars of other disciplines. As one exception, I think of J.B. Priestly's volume on the phenomenon of time.[1] A direct example of the merger is found in the conversations on aristocrats and work in Chekhov's *Three Sisters.*[2]

Further, the *use* of literature, whatever its content, invariably falls within the framework of nonwork time, and accordingly becomes an important datum in the study of the person's or the nation's leisure. An example of the first—individual leisure—is contained in a study of 26 libraries in Hillsborough County, Florida. Ada Bowen learned from a questionnaire study that:

> Of about 1200 persons over a two week period . . . the typical user is a white female, between 13–25 years of age, a student with a high school education who uses the library weekly and reads over fifteen books a year. He (or rather she) comes foremost to get a book for leisure purposes.[3]

A cross-national study of reading as a part of time-budget studies among 12 nations tells us that:

> In Torun [Poland] thirty percent of the high white collar workers, and in Maribor [Yugoslavia] fifteen percent of them, read books daily, but in Jackson [Michigan] there was not a single respondent of that category with the daily book reading habit.[4]

Thus, we have a mutual dependence: On the one hand, leisure as a whole is the primary contextual area of literature, and on the other hand, literature—both as creative writing and as reading in one's free time—is an important concern for the student of leisure. The problem then is to start with this commonality and experiment with a model for interdisciplinary inquiry that can be applied to both fields. If, indeed, a new leisure and a new language are perceived from this model, a hypothesis of considerable importance will have emerged.

For the arts as a whole, I have already selected the components of creativity, distribution, consumption, and education as the inner core of the model. The same process must take place for language and literature. Hartig and Kurz of the University of Frankfort have divided literature into the following four components:

1. The level of the inner language system (the field of linguistics)

2. The level of the medium system of language (the field of communication theory)

3. The level of the system of language use (distribution and use of language styles)

4. The level of the social system of language (language as an agent of social control).[5]

In *The Sociology of Art and Literature*, George A. Huaco employs a model around the literary phenomenon consisting of patrons, authors, critics, publishers, and audiences. All of these and others share a common purpose in trying, through our macrocosmic model, as Huaco notes:

. . . to analyze the major political, social, and economic changes in the larger society and a middle-range model to analyze the historically specific matrix of the art, film, or literature in question. The formal link between these two models is the assumption that major political, social, and economic changes in the larger society tend to affect art, literature, or film by being channeled or filtered through the social structures which constitute their social matrix.[6]

I suggest, however, that the components that apply well to analyses of leisure are equally useful for analyses of language and literature: *conditions, selection, functions,* and *meanings.*

By *condition* I mean a factor outside of the leisure or literary phenomenon that can or may determine selection, functions, or meanings within the pattern of either phenomenon. The bare listing of some factors is enough to open an immense area for common-sense observations or for more subtle studies: age, sex, place of residence, nature of one's work, amount and structure of one's time. The largest conditions are factors such as "climate of opinion," prevailing cultural values, *Weltanschauung*—which are the subject matter of the fourth level on the model. The model begins, therefore, with the most objective and measurable factors. Those in the arts and literature will find these are equally basic considerations in describing the elementary conditions which do not *determine* whether this or that person will read a book, or what type of book a person will read; but the *explanation* of her/his activity is incomplete without this fundamental data. The consequences of lack of concern for condition have been amply illustrated in the failure of some white teachers to relate adequately to black students.

The *selection* of leisure forms, including literature, is explainable in the second component, by a dynamic interplay of these objective factors with the subjective matters of will, taste, personality, mood, or whatever terms we apply, based on our views of psychology, psychiatry, philosophy, or even theology. But bringing the objective and subjective into a focus for this moment, or this day and hour, are such fortuitous intermediate factors as the weather, the bookstore display, the special television program, the advertisement, the chance meeting with a friend.

The third component, *functions,* can in both cases—leisure generally or reading as a type of leisure—be approached with traditional theories of aesthetic experience as an end or as a means of therapy, personal growth, strivings for status, or filling one's time. The ends–means explanation of functions in leisure is the basic dichotomy often applied to leisure as a whole. The Greek tradition of *paidia*—identified with Aristotelianism and updated by Sebastian de Grazia in *Of Time, Work and Leisure*—provides an aristocratically oriented view of leisure as contemplation, creativity, enjoyment of nature, or political service after the physical necessities are met.[7] The instrumentalist view of leisure is more allied to the common people, viewing it as a tool, especially for relaxation, or as recreation to prepare for more work.

For the contemporary scholar of literature in the social process, as for the student of leisure in a dynamic sense, additional tools are needed. The familiar dialectic, or the continuum within it, provides such a possibility— with such polarities to guide us as freedom and discipline, withdrawal and confrontation, or growth and entertainment.

Isaac Asimov expresses the view that space science fiction, rather than being escapist, has actually foreseen and confronted the emerging realities; *Playboy* and *Intellectual Digest* illustrate the functions of idyllic withdrawal versus reflective engagement.

An even more difficult concept is the meaning which is brought to or results from leisure experience generally or reading in particular. In addition to the usual battery of considerations which philosophy and the social sciences bring to the issue, the rapidity of change in our values has suggested the fruitfulness of an epistomology based on the classifications of assumptive, analytic, and aesthetic:

> The *assumptive* source of knowledge is the kind that reaches into past generations. It is therefore believed, affirmed, legendized, poetized, dramatized, embraced with enthusiasm, prayed to, immortalized in song, reaffirmed in salute.

> The teacher, in such a case, is the transmitter, preacher, policeman, propagandist. He reveals, reminds, and orders that which is already established. He is the guardian of the thou shalt's and the thou shalt not's. He has been delegated the authority of morality, ethical order, social control. Assumptions need not be without validity and imminent logic; they are highly important and, as far as possible, are indoctrinated to new and powerless generations of children. One thinks of religion and philosophy as preeminent models for the assumptive approach to life.

> The *analytic* source of knowledge is best illustrated by the sciences. It is a knowledge based on objectivity, evaluation, examination, doubt, tests, and experiments. Within this model one does not permit himself to be totally committed to conclusions as does a fanatic believer; he is a sort of *Luftmensch*—always stepping back from the world to look at it. Enjoyment is incidental to understanding, whether it relates to a flower, a woman, an idea, a political system, or a beautiful city such as Paris. The observer here cannot permit himself to admit "This is what I like," "This is satisfying." At least in his role as scientist, he must live out the questions: "Is it really so?", "What is it?", "How do we know?" The laboratory is one workshop for such questions, although men have made notes on the stars long ago. The case study and IBM code cards are familiar tools for the social sciences, although George Bernard Shaw did very well in his plays without either.

The educator in this type of knowledge is a fellow explorer, interpreter, midwife to the birth of new data among his students. He has no need to apply his knowledge, leaving that to his assumptive brethren; he is fundamentally an amoral man, as all social scientists must be. He is a subversive of this society and, therefore, of the educational system, for he takes seriously the half-belief that the student should be taught to think for himself.

The *aesthetic* kind of knowledge is based on the essence of originality in putting together things, objects, ideas, sounds, forms, and time and space relations in ways that have not been done before, but on the principle of beauty. It is not that creativity alone deals in symbols, for the others do so. For example, we symbolize many aspects of life, as in the prayer (assumptive) or in the hospital's antiseptic smell (an image of the analytic). The assumptive way of knowing depends for its strength on conserving, stabilizing, repeating, and ceremonializing; the strength of analytic knowledge is therefore a shock to those who cannot afford to have their notions challenged. The aesthetic attempts to view both stability and change in terms of a subjective norm through the creator's own perception and experience as a trained, sensitive, courageous, individualistic, and confident person.

Analysis and assumptions of many kinds enter into the aesthetic or creative process. But it has added a third element—subjectivity—whose essence, by definition, is that it cannot lend itself to generalization or objective verification. The nature of the aesthetic as an art is that it is undefinable in any other terms of communication or meaning known to man. This is its strength and reason for being. The educator in creative fields has the function of inducing the proper atmosphere of liberty and craft, imagination and restraint, originality and respect. He displays the masterpieces of others. He systematizes the requisite skills. He finally evokes the unpredictable resources of his students so that they may exercise their own limited perceptions of the world and thus know themselves and the world in greater depth.[8]

Using this set of tools, we can deal first with reading which is accepted as a leisure experience (no matter what is read), forming the basis for slogans one sees during "library week." It is the unstated basis for sociological data on the number of books that are read in comparison, say, to the number of visits to dog races; similarly, the expenditure figures for reading and gambling are compared, treating each as a gross activity. The next step is to move to reading which is not an abstract good, but a tangible attempt to know one's world, and finally, reading a book of Maoist writings as a way of transforming it. As an outsider to the teaching of English, I have often thought of the enormous, implicit power which such teachers have in shaping the social thought of students. A fundamental goal in any class exercises on descriptive or expository writing should be to help the student know when she/he *describes* and when she/he *proscribes*. As university students submit papers after they have interviewed families about leisure practices, I constantly find this difficulty in distinctions. What develops from it is an opportunity to guide the student toward her/his own views on the shorter work week, the guaranteed annual income, or Disneyland as a mecca for technological hedonism.

I turn now to another experiment in analysis, involving components on the model from ID (meanings), IID (nation–world), IIID (symbols), and IVD (cultivated social order).

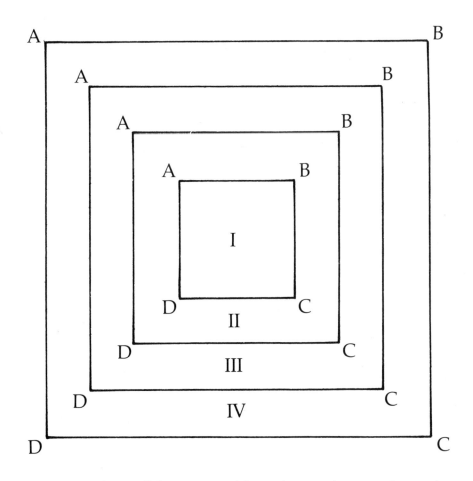

My procedure will be to proceed from the outside in, employing the musical depiction of dynamics:

, or *crescendo–decrescendo*.

The major hypothesis is that the conditions of post-industrial society, with respect to social institutions and roles, approximate a form of neo-primitivism.[9] The fusions take place over a remarkable material and technological basis for—in Sorokin's terms—something like a Sensate-Ideational reoccurrence.[10]

The implications of this for literature will become clear if we examine for a moment the meanings of this convergence. One consequence is the increasing flexibility in lifestyles, breaking away from the old pattern of childhood and youth, work life, and then retirement and death. With the four-day work week already beginning to surface, we see a new response to the desire for longer vacations, sabbaticals, and earlier retirement. It becomes possible, technologically, to think about working half a month or half a year, or half a lifetime, with retirement at age 40 or less.

It is on the level of symbolism, human values, and new vocabularies that the English-teaching field is intimately involved. Words that have been with us for centuries—work, retirement, family, old, young, play, leisure—are undergoing transformation.

The perennial issue of literature as influence or as reflection becomes pertinent in this new context. The issue of environment versus persuasion as social influences has been raised again by B.F. Skinner in *Beyond Freedom and Dignity*. Here, in its most exposed and explicit form is what used to be called "cultural determinism"; to quote the Harvard psychologist:

> As a science of behavior adopts the strategy of physics and biology, the autonomous agent to which behavior has traditionally been at-tributed is replaced by the environment—the environment in which the species evolved and in which the behavior of the individual is shaped and maintained.[11]

Mind, feeling, and, of course, persuasion of any sort are denied by this behavioral analysis. External conditions and the consequeces of past behavior become the full explanation for human behavior, and humanistic traditions attempting to explain or to control humans must give way to expanding science so that one's full freedom can be realized. I urge that you also read Noam Chomsky's pungent critique of Skinner's view of science's present and its expected future.[12]

Within the traditional statements on the functions of literature as the end and language as the tool, we recognize here the perennial dichotomy: on the one hand, literature itself as part of the environment (i.e., as an ongoing symbolic version of the ongoing reality, as one type of statement, as reflection, or as articulation); and on the other hand, literature as sufficiently outside of the environment to have an impact upon it. In the first case, English as a symbolic communication form and literature as the context are inseparable from the social environment; they are integral to the human condition, and accuracy becomes the chief criterion. Has the writer or the student of writing depicted what is, indeed, the situation? In the second case, English and literature are art forms, not repertorial tools, and as the case in all art, they are in the society but not of it; in the words of Berdyaev, all art, including literature, is sufficiently removed to comment with freedom, sufficiently integral to know intimately whereof it speaks.[13]

To the degree that literature is a persuasive influence in a period of social transition, it then has a commitment to join in the discussion on what the goals should be. There is that branch of expository literature, like Toffler's *Future Shock*, which increases our sensitivity to change and our unpreparedness for it. There are the old Utopians—from the prophets and Plato to Wells, Vonnegut, and Huxley—who produce a dramatic account of at least one alternative, desirable or not. There are the new futurists— Herman Kahn and Buckminster Fuller—who, on some scientific basis, seek to portray a "scenario" of tomorrow. And there is Isaac Asimov, who says "I told you so," and argues that science fiction must be taken not only, in its best, as excellent writing (which all of us accept) but also as a relevant clue to the world of tomorrow (an assertion which, since the walks on the moon, must be taken seriously). In other words, there is already a series of traditions in literature which have served as persuasion and depiction of the future.

The power of these literary ventures is that a serious concern with the future is not merely imaginative, nor even participative in the setting of goals. In addition, such projectivist writing has its impact on the present, for automatically questions arise: Where are we now in relation to those goals? How do we go toward them?

I am not arguing that all literature, especially among student groups, should move quite consciously toward the discussion and depiction of the future; I am noting that this desirable tendency is practically upon us, and that we can best function by realizing it. A major support for the argument comes from youth itself, whose inclination in the past decade has been precisely in these directions. Youth, as my colleague Phillip Bosserman noted:

> . . . have encountered the corporate state—the creature of the new technology and technique—the overweening bureaucracy, the objec- tification of their humanity and of others. They are not free to be independent, creative, to become what they have been extolled to be. They don't like it, can't accept it. They are convinced there is something more. They will and do wait before signing on the dotted line their contract to this corporate world.[14]

The task—indeed, the substance of the philosophy for the post- industrial, or the hopefully Cultivated society—is to bring about con- vergence of the best elements of work and leisure. From work we have such potential elements as discipline, commitment, craft and skill, responsibility, and completion of a task; from leisure we have such elements as adventure,

43

curiosity, play (in Huizinga's broad sense), and delight of discovery (in a childhood sense). I did not begin with a "definition" of leisure because we cannot begin a new task by locking it into boxes of restraining definitions. Rather, our mission is now to reopen all assumptions. We are seeking a new formulation of leisure and work to enable a more successful transition into a new era of humanity.

I conclude, therefore, that the teaching of literature will also find that its quest for interdisciplinary roots and ramifications can best succeed if it centers around a major theme, a substantive area of human life. That area already waits for widespread and mature discussion. We have the analyses of Jacques Ellul, Lewis Mumford, John Ruskin, Herbert Read, Sebastian de Grazia, Alvin Toffler, and others to provide the leads. The theme is not less than a depiction of—and, yes, a prescription for—the fusion of a material base and a nonmaterialistic value system, or of technology and humanism. We must sharpen our tools and join in an assessment of what literature has done to shape a nation in the past several hundred years, and of where it might go from here.

I have written very little directly on the actual nature of the new language that all this requires. But, more important, I have tried to suggest the new conditions—indeed, the new world—which the literature can describe and help bring about. Old terms such as "work" become less useful with the installation of each computer. During a conference on "technology, human values, and leisure," Robert Theobald said that he didn't know what those four words meant. Indeed, he noted, "I don't think any of us can define them effectively because those words are part of an industrial era language which are obsolete. Until we can create a new language, we cannot discuss our real problem—possibilities."[15] Buckminster Fuller constantly calls attention to the same need, for example, in *Utopia or Oblivion,* as he chides even the MIT faculty for continuing to use the words "up" and "down," both derived from the "milleniums in which man thought erroneously of his universe as an horizontal island," with "heaven up and hell down."[16]

We are talking, of course, not of words, as occasionally in the call for a thesaurus, but of images, of cognitive and symbolic insights which it is our responsibility to nurture into creative form, to interpret in the work of our writers, and to encourage in the communications of our students.

The basis of our interdisciplinary reachings is in part represented in psycho-linguistics or other attempts to understand communications; the quest, in part, rests on the hope that those in the field of language and literature will become more concerned with the world itself in its momentous changes.

CHAPTER 5

Personal Tensions, Leisure, and Futurology

There can be little doubt that new relationships of work to nonwork are characteristic of our time. Leisure is that portion of human experience which, within the context of free time, is a potential source of values. In all industrializing nations, roots of the new leisure are found in urbanization, in aspirations for goods, in the growth of a middle class, in an acceptance of (and at times even a victimization by) the mass media, in a desire to work less without forgoing the psychological need to be productive; there is, further, a new theology, a worldly *purgatorium,* in which we have neither Paradiso nor Inferno, but elements of both. We encounter the same issue everywhere, whether stated by Henry Thoreau, Jacques Ellul, or Eric Fromm: Does the creation of miraculous tools, such as television, imply that inevitably we become their tool? Can we maintain the best of humanistic visions and attitudes without surrendering the indubitable validity of comfort, of things, of ever new marvels in transportation and communication?

Those who would emphasize the difficulties of *forecasting* the direction of human values in this time of material abundance are asked to consider that we are unsure even of our *historical* readings. Now that the organized worker is down from a 60-hour work week to a 40-hour work week, does anyone have the tools to measure the quality of "happiness" in this gain of 20 hours each week? Alas, the computer needs to be fed before it can digest; how does one feed it the precise ingredients of happiness?

As to general descriptive data, there is now a considerable literature about the field, especially from the decade of the 1960's. Since the study has largely been preempted by sociologists, we have a rich collection of correlations of activity with such variables as age, income, and educational background. Under Joffre Dumazedier a seven-nation team is presently examining indicators of the post-industrial society. The Mouton Press has published the important 12-nation comparative study of time budgets organized by Alexander Szalai.[1] I would also call your attention, for example, to a study issued in 1972 by the Institute for the Future in the United States called *Some Prospects for Social Change by 1985 and Their Impact on Time/Money Budgets.* This Delphi study made it clear in the projections of its 27 participating experts that:

> In the aggregate, there is evidence of several related shifts in personal time expenditure. It is anticipated that the working male will spend less time at work-related activities and more time at activities related to house, home, or leisure. . . . Among those events that the panelists thought were more likely than not . . . the average (fulltime) workweek will decline to 32 hours or less . . . the average time allotted to fulltime employees for vacation will at least double; most married women will be in the labor force. . . .[2]

Thus, the empirical evidence regarding leisure is accumulating. In the broadest sweep, the new situation in more advanced industrial societies such as that in the United States may be summarized as follows:

1. Leisure is on the verge of becoming a dominant value, and one measure of the post-industrial society.

2. Leisure as a value springs from the emergence of new technological conditions, the weakening of religious supports, and the democratization of economically free time.

3. The chief technological change leading to leisure as a dominant value among the masses has been the assembly line, followed by progressive automation, with a dual impact: (1) it reduced the relative economic output of muscle in relation to machines; (2) the machine substitute tended toward an increasing impersonalization of time.

4. The Industrial Revolution, especially in its advanced stages, has removed the worker from the whole product, just as the size of the large companies has removed her/him further psychologically from an interest in the company.

5. The simultaneous industrial and marketing forces create an expertise in planning and selling a product and in programming the consumer. This expertise is converted to creating leisure goods and services to take up the slack time which was created by producing and selling assembly-line goods. Thus, the creation of time itself as a value is given substance by

the selling of things that require time to use. And *the value of work* is balanced by *the value of leisure,* both now promoted by comparable marketing techniques.

To what extent and in what degree does this outline apply only to advanced technological societies, and what are its variations among different social, economic, and occupational segments even within one society? These are pertinent questions; they have direct relevance to the meanings which leisure and work hold for persons, and they fall within a large complex of factors. While I have developed a model for this total study,[3] there is no need to summarize it here. In the model I rely on a sociological dialectic to provide a dynamic analysis which is interdisciplinary, which is qualitative as well as quantitative in research possibilities, and which views leisure as a process rather than as a mere activity. Below I shall spell out five dialectic sets which create possibilities of "tension for and against symbiosis." In each case, the tensions, as well as the prospects for personal meanings and the implications for futurologists, are identified.

First, tensions exist between the values of work and nonwork. A semi-theological contrast has been often drawn between the Christian or Puritan work ethic and the ethic of hedonism, the "fun morality": discipline as opposed to relaxation. Work, it is said, implies order, responsibility, even a semblance of divinity. Guilt is often associated with leisure, play, or amusement. Joseph Pieper attempted to dismiss these Protestant-oriented divisions, to argue that leisure can be the "basis of culture."[4] In the transition from a known work ethic to an unknown leisure ethic, the pioneers of technology—the present generations—are uncertain and hesitant.

Leisure meanings in this state of tension depend on the strength of the convictions that the person or the culture holds on the holiness of work. In the past leisure had to be "earned"; as "re-creation," its purpose was to refresh oneself for more work. The transition to the autonomy of leisure can be difficult, even with the knowledge that machines are doing more of the tasks that need doing.

Futurologists have found that the purely empirical approach cannot grapple with changing values, and hence it can hardly even conceptualize social change. Hassan Ozbekan[5] has called attention to this difficulty. Futurologists can profit from reading *The Sociology of Sociology* by Robert Friedrichs. It encourages them to move easily and with confidence from the social sciences to doses of intuition.[6] Peter Drucker pricks the bubble of surefooted predictions about technology.[7] Far more complex is the task of "pre-visions" about changing values; Beier and Rescher's collection of essays on *Values and the Future* hardly reassure one in this regard.[8] Generally, there seems to be a trend toward aspirations for "happiness," as Georges Friedmann notes, and this seems to imply both a modification of traditional attitudes toward work in the economic sense and an edging toward "works" (as in voluntary services) in the Biblical sense.

Now, we turn to the tensions between leisure as consumption and as creativity. The extensive interest in leisure by business and industry results from the growing consumer market. In the United States the official estimate is that slightly over 6 percent of all consumer expenditures are for such recreational items as tickets, mass media equipment, reading, or outdoor activity; yet, if transportation for "pleasure" is added, this proportion jumps to almost 15 percent. From the humanistic view, the time freed by technology could be useful for developing deeper values; its partisans note the access which the masses now have to creative possibilities that were once reserved for the few. Mass culture critics, following the lead of de Tocqueville and Ellul, argue that leisure, as all else, is contaminated by the quantitative and material values of "the technological society." On the personal level there is time for both—i.e., for creative opportunity or for unabashed consumption.

Leisure meanings from this perspective vary among segments of population and are affected by numerous other factors. One of the current themes of youth is a symbolic protest against the aimless accumulation of things and the work compulsion among middle-class, suburban parents. The bulk of society, undoubtedly, feels no tension at all, but goes on consuming; it is assisted in this direction by a vast advertising apparatus which, in the United States, involves many billions of dollars per year. Yet, in this same country, if the observer is not overwhelmed by naive expectations, she/he can note a steady growth in adult education, attendance at symphony concerts, wholesome outdoor activity, numbers of amateur painters, and the like.

Futurologists will do well to go beyond the familiar categories that have been constructed by sociologists in reference to social class. Increasingly, the mass media have played havoc with the identification of class through occupation or income; increasingly, lifestyles are chosen through behavioral gestures rather than ascribed by marriage or birth. Vacation patterns, the purchase of boats, and the pursuit of certain symbolic games serve as examples. The crucial issue of the future will be the cultural attitude that evolves about creativity (as in the return to handicrafts) as a respectable goal for more than the relatively few.

The tensions between going to the world and bringing the world to us emerge as two principal strands in all technological societies: Communications can provide, in McLuhan's words, a "world-village," and transportation makes map-readers of us all.[9] Television has produced the need for a new "mental ecology," for examination of the relationship of spaces as actuality and as imagery. Space must be added to time as a basic dimension of leisure; the restless urge—always in tension with the need for both psychological and physical rest—can now be indulged. Indeed, increasingly, as more societies approach the post-industrial condition, television and travel are not paradoxical but are jointly possible because of technology and increased bulk time.

Leisure meanings in both instances emphasize the feeling of freedom for the average citizen—a freedom made possible by technology. Tourists, whatever their motivations and patterns, add a new type of traveller to traditional types of the past—the missionary, the soldier, and the merchant. The point has been made that tourists are either "emphatic natives," who seek to understand the peoples whom they visit by, for example, learning their languages, or "comparative strangers," who move about in person but remain at home in terms of their attitudes and values.[10]

Futurologists will find here a rich dimension for study, especially in the fusions and interrelationships between going to the world and bringing it into one's living room via images. Witness the television-cassette systems which permit one to use images on the time schedule she/he prefers rather than according to a newspaper schedule[10]; or the growth of mass photography, which enables one to bring her/his travels back for subsequent reconsumption. As to tourism itself, a major concern for futurology lies on a semi-political level—i.e., as tourists come into cultural areas that have been relatively closed, what is the impact of the leisure of outsiders upon a previously sheltered population?

The tensions between home–neighborhood, community–region, and nation–world provide additional examples of traditions and lifestyles in relation to geographical, ecological, and symbiotic aspects. A new phenomenon in some parts of the world is the "megalopolis," which in its totality embraces the physical and cultural characteristics of many smaller entities. One example studied by Jean Gottmann is the population of 30 million along our East Coast.[11] Leisure patterns, with increased mobility and outdoor activity, serve as the bridging phenomena from inner to outer, or from the lesser to the greater of alternatives. In the United States during the 1960's the most important census finding was the move to suburban areas, indicating an attempt on the part of many to provide a daily psychological and physical bridge from the smaller to the larger circle, and to capitalize on the advantages of both urban and rural values.

Leisure meanings in this perspective fluctuate from the homogeneous to the heterogeneous, from a familiar situation to an adventure, from the relatively known to the unknown. Utilization of space outside of one's limited community requires a different type of time structure, described simply as "bulk" time, as opposed to "fragmentary" time. Since travel for extended time periods was traditionally the province of the wealthy— except for those who were preaching, conquering, or selling—the new tourism has perhaps removed the greatest symbol of wealth; leisure in this spatial sense has become a dynamic counterrevolutionary force on the one hand (outdating Veblen's concept of conspicious leisure) and a revolutionary tool on the other (through pleasure and adventure instead of violence).

Futurologists will probably find that their predictions in both domestic and international travel will be affected by the less measurable values of tomorrow and the more measurable forecasts of land and air travel. The tendency seems strongly in the direction of more travel. A circle sets in: More desire to move produces more facilities and apparatus of organization, producing in turn more desire. An example is the increase in automobile traffic which follows the increase in highways. For the cultural critic and humanist, an increasingly important issue is the potential diminution of pluralistic values as regions of the hinterland are invaded by outsiders. One of the chief values of tourism is the discovery of and emotional response to strange sights and traditions; suddenly, the perpetuation of these "oddities" becomes a financial concern for national and regional tourist bureaus, as well as a nationalistic rallying point for the residents. New balances for keeping one's relatively "primitive" area as it was, while also accommodating it to the needs of transients, will probably emerge.

Finally, tensions exist between leisure as revolution vs. counterrevolution, or as confirmation vs. innovation. A contemporary view of leisure goes far beyond the Pleasure Principle of Freud[12] or even the emphasis on relaxation found in Dumazedier.[13] The functions of leisure extend from complete fragmentation and superficiality to intensity and depth, as in the range from beach games to Beethoven. There is a place for the trivial in life, as in the reading of comic books; such acts are a corroboration of the present, and characterize the greatest portion of free-time use. Revolutionary leisure is that which potentially transforms the world or one's small part of it, as in a political act or in writing a new poem.

Leisure meanings are not inherent in such acts, but in attitudes or values brought to them. *A priori* judgments or observations by moralists or so-called scientists do not serve the purpose of realistic analysis. In a time of change—certainly, one characteristic of tomorrow's cultures—leisure, no matter how trivial, provides continuities; that is why a repetitive game of cards can be significant and an unfamiliar experience in the arts can be destructive, thus denying the validity of leisure hierarchies established by well-meaning outsiders. Familiarity and security are useful purposes in leisure. On the other hand, especially in the case of the elderly who are retired, there are dimensions of innovation and adventure that have been overlooked only because of stereotypes that originally were foisted upon everyone; as social gerontology develops enough confidence to find its paths of inquiry separate from geriatrics, the emphasis turns to inventories of accumulated experience as the basis for personal growth.[14] This provides the new outline for cultural innovation through leisure, the individual potential of which is illustrated by Charles Ives in the United States and the Russian composers who arose from the tradition-free ranks as skilled amateurs.

Futurologists must develop models that, unlike those of Utopians, are not static. It is difficult enough to project changes for the post-industrial society; it is puzzling how to inject the nature of change itself as a value. Leisure has the double possibility of creating and preventing change; this explains, in part, the active interest in this subject among socialist countries. It, thus, becomes not only an indicator of social and cultural development, but an instrument as well. To the degree that futurology provides more than a set of observations and thus becomes a bridge to national policy, the clues provided by leisure are subtle, but increasingly useful.

There are other tensions in leisure that follow from the dialectical approach of functions: leisure as reality or as symbol, as an expression of tradition or of regulation, as terminal or educational experience, as confrontation or withdrawal, as freedom or constraint, and so on. These tensions create many questions: More precisely, how are these tensions actually experienced by the person? How do various elements in the society influence a leaning toward one or the other end of the polarity? But is it not symbolic futurology itself that it properly ends in questions that are boldly drawn rather than in projections that must necessarily be humbly submitted?

CHAPTER 6

The Arts
and Recreation

It is noteworthy that President Kennedy, while dedicating what is now the Kennedy Center for the Performing Arts, said, "I have called for a higher degree of physical fitness in our nation. It is only natural that I should call, as well, for the kind of intellectual and spiritual fitness which underlies the flowering of the arts." Allowing for the need of oversimplification in the President's communication with a national public, we may take his call in its metaphorical and more contemporary sense; i.e., there is need for a sound recreational philosophy and program in our changing society; there is equal need for a concern with the arts as one creative prototype; and there is particular need to understand and act on the interrelationships between recreation and the arts.

Three fundamental questions, therefore, emerge:

1. What are the factors of change and the trends in American life that give purpose to such efforts to link recreation and the arts?

2. Considering the effects of these social and technological changes, what elements in the present state of the arts and of recreation call for a closer alliance between them?

3. What are the institutional structures, attitudes, traditions, and social processes that characterize the professional and adjunct apparatus of both fields, indicating possible areas of cooperation, natural limitations, and strategies?

Dramatic as the 200 years from 1776 to 1976 had been, there is little question of the acceleration of change that has occurred in all fields in that relatively brief period since World War II—in urban and suburban growth; transportation and communication; pure and applied technical knowledge; space exploration; educational enrollment of children, youth, and adults; general affluence; and accumulation of automatic gadgets in the home. The middle-class homeowner has continually available the energy of 85–90 "servants" in the form of push-button instant technology. In 1973 99.9 percent of all households had a black and white television; over 67.1 percent had an additional color television set. From 1950 to 1970 the total enrollment in schools among those from 5 to 34 years of age shot up from 44.2 percent to 58.9 percent. In only a half century, expectation of life for all persons at birth went up from about 54 years to almost 71 years.

In a maze of causal relationships, these measurable changes have been accompanied by transformations in social institutions and values—in family life, educational content, the church, social class structure, youth protests, expansion of government, problems of cities, struggles for better relationships between the races and justice for minorities, problems of the environment, the impact of wars, and new patterns of emotional life and personal lifestyles. Less measurable by social scientists, these changes yet come to the heart of aspirations, values, and accommodations of the new world. They are illustrated by the student who writes of the "heroin" in the opera, or by those 20 percent who annually change their residence, suffering (according to Vance Packard) from "nomadism and uprootedness." Depending on the observer's perspective and values, she/he will attribute these changes to anomie, confusion, the "new morality," crime, emotional illness, or the loss of "inner-directedness," on the one hand, or to new openness, honesty, and freedom, on the other. In both popular and serious literature there will be found a variety of interpretations. Certainly there has been a more intensive search for values and for the meanings of life itself.

Among the observations that can be made regarding this combination of material and nonmaterial changes, a few stand out due to their implications for both the arts and recreation:

1. Some observers, and notably Jacques Ellul,[1] maintain that technology has a momentum strong enough to destroy or corrupt humanistic values; hence, the question that David Riesman asks, "Abundance—for What?" is answered by "More abundance"[2]; similarly, some say that the social dislocations caused by computerization can be solved by more programming of computers. The question then becomes:

What do recreation and the arts have to say to the new "scientism"?

2. Those in the forefront of *futurology* are increasingly aware of the limitations of mere extrapolations such as population curves, and have moved toward alternative models of the future; their constructions, as in

53

Toward the Year 2000[3] or the more recent Delphi reports of the Institute for the Future,[4] now recognize the importance of human values in shaping the "post-industrial society." Toffler has translated these tendencies and forecasts into human terms of preparation for *Future Shock*.[5] Since an inherent issue, therefore, arises on the plea of traditionalism *vis-a-vis* that of modernity, or of the old *vis-a-vis* the new:

What do the arts and recreation offer in terms of cultural continuity as well as innovation?

3. A third concern which cuts across the themes noted above is the reality and consequence of "mass culture." This issue, as de Tocqueville noted, deals with the threefold destiny of creators, tastemakers, and publics under a democratized culture.[6] The issue is, in part, one of trust (or lack of trust) in the judgment of the masses, and, in part, one of lack of communication between the masses and the elites. Then:

What does the current situation with the arts and recreation say to this dichotomy in mass culture?

4. Finally, the new leisure emerges as a major issue—not as a "nonwork" time promoting attitudes that are offshoots of work attitudes and that, therefore, categorize free time actions as frivolous and peripheral; but rather as a set of actions and experiences that are increasingly central and influential, and that provide a potential source of life's meanings. The question develops:

What are the relationships of both the arts and recreation to leisure; how can the arts and recreation become integral parts of the growing research and policy formation about leisure which now concerns many nations?

Both the arts and recreation have long and honorable traditions in human history and philosophical thought. Their histories interweave, as in the cases of the upper classes whose lives were mostly given to leisure and to whom the arts were a fundamental symbol of elitism as well as a genuine interest. But they represent also a major contrast in purpose as well as in social organization.

In all forms and eras of society—primitive as well as industrial, ancient as well as contemporary—the nature and the reality of the arts have been a major issue, interest, preoccupation, and inescapable concern of all thinking persons. For if humans are distinguished by their need and ability to conceptualize the world and themselves, and to record their impressions in symbolic form, the arts are among their major forms of expression. The refinement of the arts becomes then a major criterion of human attainment. Both understanding of and creative participation in the arts have provided an historical index of social class divisions. The position of the arts has become one of the crucial clues to the inroad of scientism and impersonal technology. The usefulness of the arts to delineate the "human condition" becomes increasingly provocative. The connection of the arts, finally, to the protests and often the ambiguous searchings of our youth today is direct and important.

Over the centuries the fine arts as a whole have been associated with a relative few within any culture; these few have been identified with wealth, learning, the nobility, the clergy, or that vague and still little-understood segment called the "talented." Thus, the social structure of class, caste, and the unusual has been a central determinant. The "unusual" here are not only the talented, but also the whole range of marginal "artists" who at one time or another have comprised the performers, creators, and entertainers either of castle life in the medieval days or of television, radio, and movie life of more recent years. This restriction of the arts to the few has, in turn, resulted in a protective value by those who were actively involved; the elite felt that the true function and validity of high art had to be protected from the masses, or else the standards and functions of the arts would become diluted and cheapened.

Further, the general feeling among the elites of many societies was that *the arts constitute a part of life which is not only different but also quite isolated from, unrelated to, and—to put it crudely—"above" other aspects of life*. Art, according to this tradition, has its own history, its creators are "unique" persons, and its aesthetic values are beyond social values. This separatist attitude went hand in hand with the class structure; it found its expression in the kinds of people who gravitated toward the arts and, conversely, in the suspicion of artists and their world which developed among broad masses of population.

A third observation: the philosophical positions on aesthetics have varied in the same way as have philosophical positions in general—from rationalism, idealism, or positivism to the various degrees of existentialism; but in general, *the arts have usually been drawn as a contrast or at least as a commentary upon reality as a whole*. Such terms as "escape" or "withdrawal" may be old-fashioned, but they suggest this premise. Economically and socially we have not known how to deal with the arts. We ask, for instance, is it "real" work that has gone into the painting, and what is its worth? Is the artist really "with it" as she/he goes her/his own way, forfeiting the comforts which any "practical person" wants in exchange for ideals, freedom, and independence from the social norms which good middle-class Americans should adhere to? But perhaps that is the point: Do artists belong to the normal pictures which we have drawn for the banker and the plumber, or for upper-middle, lower-middle, upper-lower, lower-upper . . . ? A more complete profile would have to deal with historical eras, differences between the arts, stratification within each art, and the like.

The tradition of art deals primarily with *symbolic expression;* people are involved, but they are secondary. From this, we turn to the "tradition" of recreation. Recreation emphasizes *people;* symbols such as social class are involved, but secondarily. The time for recreation has traditionally been nonwork time, and the concept of play, amusement, recreation, or leisure has always been built around the work idea, even for the rich. The work was done for the Greek aristocrats who were then free to debate justice on a corner of Athens or in the Academy.

From work, especially after the rise of Christianity, came not only one's goods and services but also one's identity, one's purpose in life. The arts, on the contrary, have long been characterized as outside the realm of productive work. It may be that the profession of recreation has for a long time been misnamed, for re-creation, a getting ready for work, is peculiarly a term to be applied to the adult world; the child's world, technically, is that of *play;* play, if we accept Huizinga's classical discussion, is its own world of order, with its own play*ground* or locus, its own organic structure and experience.[7] Play is an *end*—although its content may have instrumental implications; *recreation as preparation for a return to work has been historically a means, but it becomes increasingly an end as the worker—Homo Faber—becomes outdated, and the adult player—Homo Ludens—takes over.*

A second characteristic of adult recreation, as well as of children's play, has been that *our many cultures have attached social values to it.* These values have been of two types. One type is identified from the specific activity, so that from a football unit we get not only a team but also additional morality in the term "team play" or in such interesting contrasts as "fair" and "foul" play. The second type of value is a morality not inherent *in* the action but *about* the action, such as who may play with whom. Here the crucial factors historically have been the symbols of social distinctions and identities— classes, castes, minorities, the "teen-age" culture, children's games, women's games, and so on.

Yet although there are values *in* recreation and values which *surround* the contexts of recreation, these values have originated not from or through recreation, but in such traditional institutions or arrangements as work, family, ethnic groups, the church, the state, the business or economic world, or various political ideologies. Here again there is a contrast with the aesthetic, for while aesthetic theory has long held that the arts are more than paintings or plays or literature, and that they all represent a unique source of knowledge and a way of viewing the world, *there has been a less comparable body of philosophical tradition about recreation.* This may be fortunate for our present moment in history, for the dramatic changes of our time make deep inroads upon the theories and practices of the arts; recreation, refreshingly free from inner cults, fights, and academic struggles, can more directly face the world of dramatic change.

The social and technological changes in the first three-quarters of this century have seriously upset the familiar images of both the arts and recreation. The direction has been to bring each closer to the other.

As to the arts, there was a time before WPA when government assistance was neither available nor wanted; the example of the USSR, with its dangers of control, was fresh. Again, after World War II artists, happily off the welfare rolls, opposed using the arts as "propaganda" but seized the opportunity to go abroad for the United States. Another influence toward new thought on the arts in society came from the artist-in-residence posts and the flowering of all the arts on the American college campus, extending a strong movement that was familiar in the high schools; the college campus provided congenial colleagues, stimulating students, faithful audiences, and welcome salaries from Tallahassee to Ann Arbor to Los Angeles. The press of urban problems, especially after the wave of race riots, introduced the most dynamic of current changes in attitudes toward and about the arts, under the leadership of such creators as Budd Schulberg and Katherine Dunham. The Brooklyn College seminar in 1967 reported the actual or potential influences of the arts in the ghetto setting in terms of confidence, taste, discipline, nonverbal expression, mental health, interpersonal relations, perceptual skills, constructive social action, sense of accomplishment, self-discovery, ethnic identity, and personal uniqueness. In addition, the arts in such a setting were found to be far more at home in the "recreational" than in the traditional "educational" milieu.[8]

Thus, the major advantages which the arts can gain from a close relationship to recreation are:

1. To make more explicit the social functions of the arts relating to identity, therapy, and personal growth;

2. To relate the arts more explicitly and systematically to new audiences (such as retirement groups, the handicapped, and the hospitalized) and to new settings and facilities (such as community centers, parks, and camp situations);

3. To uncover creative possibilities within groups not ordinarily in direct contact with the arts;

4. To utilize both the organizational skills and experiences that are an integral part of the recreation and park professions on the local or county level, and the professional apparatus of these professions on regional, state, national, and international levels;

5. To coordinate research in such areas as architectural developments, group dynamics, personality needs, sources of cultural innovations, and so on.

Social and technological changes have served to broaden the theoretical perspectives of the recreation profession, as presently reflected in the forward-looking curricula of some university training programs. Research in the field has become more serious and skilled, leading to a *Journal for Research in Leisure*. Over the years, while physical activity continued, recreational programming moved into the arts, travel experiences, volunteerism in the community, and special services to such segments as the handicapped and the elderly. Long before the public schools thought they had discovered the "free" school, summer camps were already experts in programmatic freedom. Such pioneers as Charles Brightbill helped conceptualize the broadened horizon of recreational functions,[9] and Siebolt Frieswyk had spoken for the arts within the National Recreation and Park Association.

The realization began to grow that whatever had been achieved by the recreation profession in the past half century had been introductory to the new demands upon it, and that the maturation of its responsibilities meant an alliance with all community agencies and many relevant academic disciplines, a concern with the full lifestyle and family life of the public, and an interweaving with the full range of thinking in the leisure field. As the arts had always thought and acted on an international level, so recreation in the United States became aware of European and Oriental traditions of play and uses of time through conferences, publications, and visitations. New segments of the population, such as the elderly, were rediscovered. Playgrounds and community centers continued to serve their purposes, while parks, industrial settings, churches, apartment complexes, homes, and even prisons and hospitals also came to be utilized as natural stages for the free, creative play of young and old, ill and well, novitiate and expert.

Thus, the major advantages that the recreation profession can gain from a close relationship to the arts are:

1. To have ongoing access through official sources to the enormous complex of the various arts, including their institutional structure, professional organizations, leadership, training programs, and so on.

2. To obtain direct advice and knowledge from within the community in locating performing or teaching groups and individuals and in determining the conditions under which they are available in the recreational setting.

3. To engage leaders from the arts who represent professional standards but who also bring to bear a knowledge of persons and groups.

4. To expose recreational users to experiences in the arts that permit a maximum of creative as well as personal growth.

5. To enlarge the total recreational philosophy and practice with more authoritative leadership and consultation in a large area which has something to say on the matter of social directions in the changing society.

Some general observations on the possible areas of cooperation between the arts and recreation may serve as useful guides for the future.

The major traditional characteristics of the arts and of recreation must be understood and respected; the value of each to the other evolves directly from their respective preoccupations with the aesthetic and the social. For example, the recreational stress on the "amateur" will continue to ward off some segments of "professional" art; conversely, the natural concern of the latter with standards will be respected by recreation leaders who, nevertheless, are committed to principles of open participation and human exchange. These distinctions cannot be argued; they represent legitimate directions. Cooperation is something less than conquest, and is based on the application of respective contributions in a given situation.

A primary focus on the rapport between the arts and recreation can be within the community but outside of the traditional settings of school, community center, or concert or exhibition hall. The time is ripe for the invention of new agencies and settings which meet the needs of all ages, and in which the general community becomes involved in planning and policy. Urban park areas have hardly been tapped for their potential in the synthesis of the creative, the natural, and the human. Architects are among those who need to become aware of architectural and recreational trends; special attention might also be given to innovative planning for the arts and recreation in new communities for retirees and for mixed agencies utilizing public and private funds.

The inner city provides a provocative and promising setting for creative interplay of the arts and recreation. For previous generations of ghetto-dwelling minorities, the arts served as a means of achieving social acceptance, Americanization, and contact with the "other world"; the present inner city, populated mostly by blacks and Chicanos, is more concerned with finding its "inner" identity. In either emphasis, the arts and such recreational forms as historical study or volunteer service are providing both a continuity with the past and an exploration of the future. Here are to be found new sounds, theatrical forms, fresh audiences, and innovative combinations of folk and fine art. Recreation, like education, seeks new paths in the essential task of freeing itself from middle-class white practices that may be ineffective.[10]

Numerous issues will confront recreation and the arts in the attempt to relate both to the educational practices of the community. Within the American school system, the arts, especially the performing arts, have already developed beyond the educational tradition of many other nations. Also, the use of school facilities for recreational purposes has increased rapidly in the United States. A third factor that is relevant, especially within the past decade, is the prevalence in many schools of instruction in such areas as rock music, "stage bands," and folk songs and dances. Therefore, the problems we face involve a three-way relationship. Similar, but less frequent cross-relationships will be found in those communities with forward-looking adult education programs. Thus, as the communications between the arts and recreation are increased, both fields, separately and collectively, will find it necessary to communicate more actively with other components of the community, such as education, labor, business, church, and government.

Among the several major segments of the population to whom special attention might be given are the elderly. Of the 22.4 million Americans over 65 — one in every ten — many have already been touched by recreational, park, and art programs. Yet much remains to be done, in light of our failure as a nation to respect their accumulated experience and their potential for creative growth. The booklet *Older Americans and the Arts,* prepared by Jacqueline Tippett Sunderland[11] for the National Council on Aging and the John F. Kennedy Center for the Performing Arts, notes the social value of the arts, offers numerous illustrations of current programs, suggests valuable approaches to programming, and lists numerous resources for information on aging and the arts. It can serve as a stimulating and practical guide to programs which might be attempted for other segments of the population as well.

Finally, the effort to develop a rapport between the arts and recreation is bound to fail if its objective is no more than the search for piecemeal, for isolated bits and pieces, based upon practices already familiar and upon an attempt by each field to preserve its integrity from the other. Rather, the mood and intent must be positive, based upon a conviction that the purpose and function of each are expanded as a common effort affects more persons more deeply than they are now. Any program must, therefore, go far beyond programmatic strategies (important as these may be for services and visibility) into common research, joint training plans, and ongoing communications. Working together, these two fields can better prepare to offer their respective values to a society experiencing rapid change. Together, the arts and recreation suggest new sources of human values for individuals, families, neighborhoods, and segments within the larger community.

CHAPTER 7

Leisure,
Human Values,
and Religion

It is possible to view the string quartet as the perfect aesthetic tool for much great music. The quartet is also a classic social prototype—a model of one *vis-a-vis* the group, simplicity within diversity, homogeneity and heterogeneity. Thus, the structure here will consist of four subjects, each a complex theme that presents a fundamental paradox or interplay within itself, and all interrelated, if not always harmoniously.

Theme One: Just when leisure studies have matured under the discipline of sociology, its issues explode into problems of values. Leisure, as a still undisciplined adolescent about 15 years old, asks the difficult questions: Why? What for? Is it good? Is it destructive?

Theme Two: As moral issues become central to the subject of leisure, and as religion turns its attention in this direction, heaven has become secularized, transplanted to the suburban environment, transformed into a symbol of materialistic content or comfort.

Theme Three: An intellectual ambiance develops to provide a sympathetic hearing for earth-oriented values, but it is unable to provide a much-needed humanistic philosophy and turns to the negativism of anti-technology and anti-growth.

Theme Four: What was formerly the area of study least likely to generate intellectual respect in the university—recreation, health, physical education—finds itself in less than two decades holding major clues and insights for the post-industrial order, inviting the humanists and social scientists to share its visions for the social transformations ahead.

The moral dimension of leisure is its most significant current characteristic. At issue is not the amount of time free from productive work;

Wilensky notes that the Middle Ages had more free time.[1] It is not the so-called contemporary patterns of sabbaticals and flexitime, for primitive peoples often display a spontaneous adaption to mood. The fact of our time is an attitude toward work as an instrument and not as an orchestration of life's meanings. The divinity of work *per se,* long a tenet of Christianity, capitalism, and Marxism, seems to give way. Studies such as the Department of Health, Education, and Welfare's *Work in America* document the change.[2] Fred Best has reviewed much available data to conclude, in a private study for HEW, that over the past century, the American worker has increasingly chosen more free time over more income.[3] Note the recent labor negotiations that reject provisions for compulsory overtime.

Here we are faced with a double philosophical and psychological transformation: the diminishing of work as the major source of moral responsibility and the elevation of the moral potential in leisure. Sociology of the Western, positivistic tradition is unable to cope with this transformation. Surely there are statistical components of the inquiry, for it remains imperative that we investigate who is doing what, but the "why's" are hardly answerable in these typical academic correlations. Sociological or scientific accuracy of data is not to be mistaken for significance of findings. A refreshing treatment of the subject is provided by the Rapoports in *Leisure and the Family Life Cycle.*[4] They raise moral issues in an analysis of children, young adults, the establishment phase, and retirement. The Rapoports are social psychologists with anthropological and psychoanalytic backgrounds; equally interesting, these English scholars come from a mixed capitalistic/socialistic framework of culture and thought. In Iran I have seen another mixed economy, one that is struggling to find a cultural balance between its rapid progress toward industrialization due to its "petro-dollars" and its traditions from a rich Islamic history. Thus, for Iran's national planners leisure has suddenly become a major clue or indicator of a moral balance between the old and the new, between the culture of yesterday and that of tomorrow. There, as well as in western Europe, the socialistic nations, and the United States, a common value has emerged—not in the political or economic realm, but in the universal quest of the masses for purpose beyond maintenance, for survival beyond longevity, and for personhood beyond mere existence.

Surely, if a positivistic social science is uniquely disqualified to deal in depth with an issue of values, religion should be permanently ready. Is not the social message of all religions grounded in ethical teachings, in the emphasis on purposes and ends? But religions differ in the historical relation of their ethical theory to economic scarcity and abundance. For moral truth cannot be separated from available means for its attainment. Nor is insecurity—psychological, social, material—unrelated to earthly deprivation and other-worldly aspiration. Thus, for example, the ancient

Stoic philosophy put complete emphasis on the mind, for thought is always a potential accumulation open to all, independent of the material world. More recent ethics, notably in Jeremy Bentham, develops a pleasure theory based on industrial expansion, optimism, and abundance. Marxism comes fully to an ethic based on abundance for all as a political–economic–theological faith, substituting earthly goals for heavenly promises. Existentialism focuses on the individual, thereby substituting psychology for morality, and a concept of heaven is then unnecessary. As for Christianity, its social origins are rooted in the idea of a heaven that was powerful enough to balance off the deprivations on earth. Paradoxically, it was the Judaic tradition—perhaps more accurately, the Jewish community ethos—grounded on a perennial struggle for survival, that defined its heaven as paradise on earth; thus, the strong emphasis on optimism, on the legitimacy of job, and on the sensual and mental pleasures as integral values. Even in Israel today, one finds mature discussions about creative life as its border guards hitch-hike home from outposts of lurking death to attend cultural events.

Thus, as economic scarcity has given way to the expectation of widespread abundance, Christianity seems to have cooperated with the profane institutions in the physical-psychological-cultural-theological relocation of heaven to earth. Paradise has achieved instant visibility and attainability through the dispensers of television specials and sports, through Florida winter vacations, or through whatever the impatient person wishes to associate with her/his heavenly quest. Perhaps the church could not meet the challenge. After all, can the pulpit's vague visions match the pragmatic paradisiac palpitations provided by *Peyton Place?*

But, indeed, the church can affect this relocated secularized heaven if it embraces the issue of leisure as a whole—as a source of values, not as a value in itself. For then it can deal with the panorama of mass media entertainment, the serious arts, education, sports, sociability, and public service as an interrelated whole, symbolizing the human soul and psyche at their best. On lower and more immediate levels of recreation as a strategy, the church is on familiar grounds. In *The Church as a Social Institution,* David Moberg notes that church activities have always had manifest and latent recreational consequences for individuals and society.

> Religious art, ritual and pageantry, church music, symbolic pictures in the scriptures, messages by fluent preachers, literature in church publications, church-related social gatherings, fraternizing before and after church services and even inquisitions against the enemies of religion have provided recreational gratifications. . . .[5]

Professor Moberg also recalls for us that new "functional equivalents"—such contemporary provisions as gymnasiums, lounges, and drama clubs—have taken the place of such traditional events as suppers and ice cream socials. But only the outward appearance has been changed. The traditional and immediate purposes remain, even though more formality is evident. As other community facilities have developed—community centers, public golf courses, etc.—the church opposition to them has declined, and it has even encouraged or taken over commercial aspects, such as bingo games. It is true, as Moberg concludes, that religious conflict has arisen from differing attitudes about recreation and the recognition in some quarters that the church had missed the opportunity to develop a true synthesis of the saintly and the social.

When the Universalist–Unitarian merger took place, I proposed that the union—and all churches, in fact—could fruitfully turn to the most legitimate relationship that now awaits the common interest of all churches: that is, leisure as a new source and center of human growth. In one stroke, all of the surface devices listed by Moberg could be justified; indeed, they could be amplified, observed, and made the subject of significant analysis.

Only a few in the church—Harvey Cox and Gordon Dahl[6] among them—have followed these leads.

The values that the church can discover and develop in leisure cannot, I submit, ignore the phenomenon of technology, such as the excitement that television can produce. This is the third paradox, mentioned at the beginning and discussed further below. The values that religious tradition can bring into the discussions on leisure or into its own policies and programs need not be negative. For the leisure activities that are actually being experienced cover an enormous range from fishing and writing poetry to gliding and playing checkers. Although the unending itemization can be placed into classifications, church leaders face a serious danger at this point, i.e., confusing the necessity for assigning social or even spiritual values with the assumption of a hierarchy of values in leisure. This was the mistake made during the first national conference on leisure that I have been able to trace—one that took place in Boston over 20 years ago, sponsored by the Jewish Theological Seminary. Then, very much as Joseph Pieper had done earlier in *Leisure: The Basis of Culture* for the Catholic position,[7] physical activities were given a lower ranking than prayer, study, or use of the mind. There will surely be no quicker road to disaster for the church in this field than to assume that its absolution in the theological realm can, as a technique of persuasion or as an arbiter of human action, be applied to the leisure experience. *For whereas the basis of Christian theological thinking derives from accepted universal principles that supersede the personal condition, leisure in contemporary Western life—grounded in both a material abundance and a democratic ethos of the choice—derives from the dignity of the individual.* Regretfully, the humanistic tradition outside of the church is not providing the social philosophy that is needed to buttress the church's awakening.

Perhaps the most surprising aspects of our intellectual community have been its persistent attacks on technology; its subscription to the gloom of Heilbronner, Ellul, Illich, Mumford, Sorokin, and Toynbee; and, therefore, its failure to articulate our national or pan-national goals. Has vision for the future died with H.G. Wells, Sidney Webb, and Edward Bellamy? Have humanistic philosophers been silenced by our computer-oriented futurologists—by Herman Kahn and the Club of Rome? Have we forgotten that our dreams and aspirations have impact on our policies and hence our destinies? It is useful to raise questions about our cultural directions and to wonder whether the work ethic has been one of our major myths, useful for the ideology of the happy worker, just as during the early part of the Industrial Revolution, social Darwinism proved itself a useful myth for the happy employer.

Presently, the so-called work ethic is becoming the basis of a prevalent gloom among those humanists who see no hope for creative leisure. The esteemed Georges Friedmann, the French industrial sociologist, quite properly expressed the familiar defeatism several decades ago, but his analysis remains where it was then. More recently, Dr. Jack Weinberg, a Chicago psychiatrist, once again paraded all the Calvinist virtues of work in a mid-career conference sponsored by our University—I thought I was hearing John Calvin and Calvin Coolidge. This type of rallying cry goes along with the humanists' certainty that we are a materialistic society; yet annually we spend $6 million more going to the arts than to all professional sports. True, we continue to watch television in almost every home—and in color in 67.1 percent of our homes—but the use of our libraries has also risen, even among children. We have been experiencing inflation, and an unemployment rate more than twice that of any western European nation; yet, as *U.S. News and World Report* noted in 1972, the total sum spent that year for leisure exceeded our total expenditure for national defense or for the construction of new homes, or the total of corporate profits, or the aggregate income of all farmers, or the overall value of our exports.[8] We have too many poor people, perhaps 20 percent among our 214 million; yet according to reliable studies of the 20th Century Fund, the average home has enough built-in energy (heater, refrigerator, washing machine, etc.) to equal 85 or 90 servants throughout the 24 hours, relieving its occupants of such chores as carrying water and coal, lighting kerosene lamps, or even washing dishes.

As to the general current mood, many observers find now a certain cynicism within our country, a suspicion of politicians and lawyers, a decreasing confidence in education, science, and business. Such groups as blacks, women, the young, and the elderly are affirming their independence from traditional stereotypes about how they *should* act and what they *should* expect from life. One of our well-known commentators, Bill Moyers, a former assistant to President Johnson, stated on a national broadcast, "What gives you real choice in our society is money. Democracy in effect says equal rights. Capitalism in fact delivers unequal results." And the Gallup poll reported in 1977 that there has never been a time during its 40-year existence when its surveys have found the population to be so pessimistic. Finally, Daniel Bell sees in the current American mood a feeling of alienation in that for most of human history, "reality was nature," then "reality became technics," and now, the post-industrial society is "essentially a game between persons."[9]

These feelings, no doubt, were caused or fed in part by Vietnam and Watergate, by the civil rights struggle, and by the defection of youth in the 1960's. Yet, the leisure phenomenon cautions us about these interpretations. Are these measures of pessimism or political estrangement too close to the surface? Or do they suggest a more fundamental transformation in our values and our cultural patterns?

What the humanist critics are failing to see is that the significant trends toward increasing leisure—even in times of adversity—are not based on a sort of fatalism, or existentialism, or "escape," or other form of national therapy. Rather, our increasing preference for free time—longer weekends, vacations, sabbaticals, earlier retirement—is a natural emergence from our history and from a maturation of our purposes.

As far back as the 1870's, labor unionists had set as their goal the eight-hour day. This was not to be fully realized for 60 years, but by the 1920's, the great technological growth had begun. Immigration had stopped after World War I. More mechanization became essential—and profitable as the output went up; but because unions were still weak, workers did not generally get the benefit of the expansion. Women became an important addition to the labor force, but they were hard to organize because of the attitudes that until recently had prevailed, i.e., an attitude of the temporariness of work and a willingness to accept less money than men for the same work. At that point the shorter working day was not promoted as a means to increase leisure, but rather as a device to distribute work among more people as unemployment rose during the Depression of the early 1930's. Workers were employed about 50 hours per week when Henry Ford's dramatic policy of the five-day week was announced in 1926. Paid vacations were practically nonexistent for the workers, if not for the managers.

Following the election of Franklin Roosevelt in 1932, a series of revolutions created the legal and ideological basis which supports today's employees. The 40-hour week became the basis of Roosevelt's reforms, with overtime to be paid at 50 percent more. Leisure consumption patterns were affected in the economic recovery; for example, 23,000 movie houses were established by 1939. From one radio station in 1920 the number grew to 600 by 1940. The public works programs—PWA, WPA, CCC, and others—were effective under Roosevelt in the 1930's. Aside from providing employment, these programs created a vast network of playgrounds, parks, and leadership in the arts as well as in sports and games; symphony orchestras, operas, and theaters were created to set a pattern for a cultural growth that is still present. The leisure of unemployment proved in the Depression to be an unwanted and false free time; even now, decades later, we see the same phenomenon. But one further accomplishment of the 1930's—the passage of our Social Security Act—created an economic base for the retired, thus establishing for the elderly a fundamental distinction between retirement and unemployment.

The decades of the 1940's, 1950's, and 1960's saw enormous technological advances. The number of televisions per 1,000 persons increased from 70 sets in 1950 to 322 sets in only 12 years. The post-war economy provided the common family with its car, its refrigerator, its access to a world of comfort, services, and distances that in the past was conceivable only by the rich—or even beyond them.

By 1970, the average work week in the United States was down to 40 hours; the labor unions were negotiating for two to three weeks of paid vacation; and among our 28 million over the age of 60, 6 of every 10 were fully retired. And of the retirees, the majority of men would live long enough into their seventh decade that over the full lifetime, they would have as many hours at leisure as at work.

By the 1970's also, a large array of leisure alternatives was available to the masses, from the 27 million who attended baseball that year to the 68 million who watched and bet on horseracing to the almost 10 million who saw Broadway shows.

This level of leisure activity was inevitably accompanied by, caused by, or, in any event, related to decisive changes in our family, work, and community patterns. One example was the opportunity, created by federal legislation, to enjoy five weekends of three days each, by moving various national holidays to a Friday or a Monday. Families became more flexible in the relationships of husband to wife and of parent to child. The so-called revolution in morals became apparent, and various communal forms of living became acceptable. Especially during the early days of the energy crisis, communities found that less driving of cars put a new strain on local parks and community centers. Yet, although many trips are shorter, a *New York Times* summary, dated July 20, 1975, concluded that more Americans were traveling to national parks, seashores, and resorts than in the previous year. The marketing manager of Disney World in Florida told me that the number of 1976 visits was 11 percent higher than the number made by this time in 1975. DATA (Discover America Travel Association) discovers that the desire to travel is ingrained, and people in 1977 are willing to pay higher prices if they know what the cost will be in advance.

In the broadest sense, the American masses have become increasingly interested in more time to explore their interests, and more skilled in pursuing those interests that require more time. We cannot set priorities for the time of others; a happy situation for a free leisure is that while 20 million of us attend weekly classes of some kind, one of every eight persons between the ages 14 and 44 bought a bicycle last year; and our bars and houses of prostitution are not suffering for business either.

On the matter of our values in American life as revealed through leisure, again a profound change has been occurring. Its origins go beyond the youth movement of the 1960's. In that decade, for example, eight million persons moved from the colder northern states to the warmer and slower lifestyles of the southern states. Our population in Florida doubled in that period. Of course, the transformation goes beyond physical comforts, sunshine, golf, or beaches. More profound change can be approached by the juxtaposition of three religious traditions: Christianity, Judaism, and Confucianism.

The Christian values of work, frugality, and the hoped-for heaven have continued among us, but this ethic has not prevented us from adopting technology in production, business, or the home: Computers have grown from 2,000 in 1959 to 170,000 in 1975; vacuum cleaners and other labor-saving devices are found in practically every home.

The Judaic sense of proportion has been adopted by us in bringing the "good life" into the daily levels of faith and fact. No trace of spiritual guilt is to be found among the 90,000 New Yorkers who occasionally hear their symphony perform in Central Park.

Finally, especially from observations among our active older persons, one sees the Confucian principle of personal growth in our post-industrial lifestyles. The scholar Tu Wei-Ming tells us that ". . . the idea that one's life on earth can and should be differentiated into discrete modes of existence and is, in essence, a preparation for an afterlife does not seem to have occurred in the Confucian tradition. The emphasis instead is on the process of living itself."[10] This is far different from hedonism; for the evolving American leisure pattern is in good part devoted to transitory and empty activities, but it also includes significant examples of self-growth.

Never before in its two centuries has the United States provided such favorable objective conditions for every type of activity–experience or for every segment of its population—old or young, rural or urban, rich or poor, blue or white collar worker, well or ill, male or female. It is not a classless society, and major disparities in opportunity exist. The fact that commercial entertainment dominates the consuming scene is self-evident. Yet the growth of public facilities is evident, as in our parks, libraries, schools, and community centers.

This democratization of the physical base has also helped to level our lifestyles through leisure, or at least to open the possibilities of flexibility and individual choice to the largest portion of our citizens. Social status among us—perhaps among other societies as they industrialize—is increasingly determined on an individual basis of choice and accomplishment rather than by circumstances of class. Yet the criticisms of mass culture continue as the intellectual community, absorbed with its critical role, fails to offer a program and philosophy for the latter part of this century based on our national strengths and potentials. But what of the intellectual community within the American university itself? Should this not be our primary source for analyses of leisure and human values and the foundation of goals?

You will recall the final proposition, that the foundation for the new philosophy is led in the American university by spokespersons who formerly enjoyed the least status—physical educators and recreationalists—now pulling the humanists and artists into their folds.

There were reasons for sociologists to take an early lead in the new study, for leisure was always seen as an offshoot of work. Simple questions quickly arose: How much free time does the worker have? What does she/he do with it? How do such factors as income and education correlate with types of nonwork activity? These were standard issues. However, through the 1950's and into the 1960's most sociologists ignored leisure as a subject for serious study. Perhaps more surprisingly, it was ignored even among those who specialized in family life. Psychologists have begun to consider the subject, as have a few psychiatrists including Reid Martin and Karl Menninger. Anthropology had always incorporated play and art as integral aspects of primitive society. A few economists—Lindner in Sweden and Owen in the United States—have written with insight. Philosophers, notably Pieper, found here a fundamental diagnosis of civilization. Philosophy departments of American universities have remained unheard on leisure issues. The arts avoided the subject, viewing amateurs as dilutors of their standards.

Yet, there was a campus contingent that, by its commitments and skills, was directly concerned with leisure on a daily basis. A lack of adequate conceptualization was to be expected in the growth from a preoccupation with the body and theories of play to a concern with community and society. Budgets, credits, and curricula were often justified more on the basis of recreational clichés than on rational analysis.

It is surely too much to ask these departments to assume more than an educational role within the university. As I pointed out in a series of essays brought together by Diana Dunn, the strongest allies of our recreation and leisure departments are those forces outside the campus who are committed to orientating new lifestyles for themselves—youth, women, the elderly, and blacks. This means, however, a move toward an integration among the values of human growth (Confucian), of mind and service (Judaic), and of commitment to tasks (Christian). It implies a large interest among the students of departments in the social sciences, in philosophy and history, in personality development, in national directions. Are they ready to take this larger stage?

Unless the lead is taken by the universities, I fear for their role as an intellectual or moral guide for the decades ahead. Everywhere, with budgetary squeezes, state legislatures are asking for marketable courses and skills. Many educational systems are now at the point where professors have to submit a justification for every course, and many, no doubt, will be eliminated. Next up for the marketplace requisition will be curricular programs. Church and university bring together two strands of thought and power. And such policies set the directions of our strategy and, more, the type of cooperation most fruitful for the emergence of a philosophy and a creative leisure for the cultivated society.

CHAPTER 8

The Urban Framework for New Work and Leisure

Shortly after the turn of the century my parents and many others came from Lithuania during a period—from 1880 to 1915—when over 30 million immigrants arrived. These immigrants came to Milwaukee from many countries—more from Germany than from elsewhere—for adventure, for a better life, for freedom from famine and pogroms. Those who came to pick gold off the streets often found instead that they had to build the streets, as well as the factories and the cities.

In other eras as well, heterogeneous populations have been attracted to the cities, leading (as Plato observed) to innovation. The complexity of backgrounds and motivations has made the city a traditional setting for dualities in function. On the one hand, there is the working life, and on the other, there is the more general and amorphous social, intellectual, and recreational life; the latter goes beyond the factory, bank, store, stock market, school, and office of the mayor, to such facilities as the library, symphony hall, park, church, and home. It is an oversimplification to speak of the urban community as a functional synthesis of means and ends, work and nonwork, business and pleasure; but in reality we do indeed refer in the vernacular to this distinction—the city as a place to "work" and a place to "live."

It is further apparent that sometimes the facilities and perceptions related to "working" and "living" reinforce each other, and sometimes there are serious conflicts. Examples of the former exist where the size of the city permits the arts as well as opera and major educational institutions to flourish; an example of the conflict occurs where tourists bring money into an area, but by bringing themselves they add to the crowding, the pollution, and the traffic. There is this constant struggle and reassessment between the preservation of the old or the beautiful and the so-called "progress" brought about as new needs arise.

On the physical level, one consequence has been a European Conference of Ministers which met in Brussels under the auspices of the Council of Europe. Their report called *Past in Future* notes that:

> In truth there is no conflict between yesterday's creations and the achievements of today; they are of necessity complementary. The integration of our immovable cultural property with contemporary and future civilization is a necessity for its harmonious development . . . to satisfy man's physical and spiritual needs.[1]

The report also notes the political nature of this problem, to create the conditions for "a new humanism."

Yet the essence of the conflict or the reinforcement goes much deeper than physical beauty, architecture, or the location of new roads. The basic character of these two poles—"working" and "living"—is undergoing profound change in fact and in perception. And it is these changes that may mark a turning point not only in the priorities or values of emerging generations in all industrial societies, but also in the issues they raise regarding the city's future in the so-called post-industrial society.

As to work, the past 50 years have witnessed numerous and dramatic changes. Domestic industry and small manufacturing units have developed into large industry and complex factories. Populations have been attracted to expand the industrial output from far places within the nation, and as here since World War II, from other nations as well. A management and sales apparatus for the organization and distribution of goods has created the characteristic inner city. Overcrowding and serious problems of ghettos or slums emerged in many areas, such as Mexico City, New York, and Johannesburg. Pollution became a natural consequence of unplanned growth. Social class distinctions became manifest in both physical and social levels. Such writers as Lewis Mumford, Ebenezer Howard, and the Bauhaus founders criticized the city and offered a creative philosophy for rebuilding and replanning. The wars in Europe, tragic as they were, stimulated new planning of necessity. Economic revitalization of the past quarter century in Germany has further enhanced radical innovation along both physical and social lines. At present in Japan, in good part as a response to the world's worst environmental and pollution crisis, a national policy for decentralizing industry is being executed by cooperative efforts of government and big business.

Meanwhile, the electronic or cybernetic revolution in all technological societies has transformed the nature of work itself.

Computerization is the fastest growing, and by 1980 may be the largest of all industries. In the United States, we had 2,000 computers in 1959, and now we have 170,000; in western Europe, their number in the same period went from 265 to 110,000; in Japan, from 11 to 41,000 computers in 15 years. Automation and other production techniques have produced a growth rate in the United States' total economy that has risen from 3.8 percent in 1950 to 5.9 percent in 1972. Our work week has declined from 60 hours to 40 since the turn of the century. In part, the displacement of workers by machines has swelled the proportion of workers in the service areas, and since 1956 more American workers have been in services than in manufacturing or farming, providing Daniel Bell with one of his criteria of the post-industrial society.

In between these technological or economic changes on the one hand and this transformation of lifestyles on the other hand came the miracles of new transportation and communications which we discussed in Chapter 5. Already the city had been a bridge to the rest of the world, but now the television brought other city characteristics to rural and semi-rural populations. Among these leisure elements were traditionally the variety of persons and facilities as well as the association of city existence with "life" and "excitement." Der Kurfurstendamm and the Champ de Elysses are distinctly urban leisure romances, and the accessibility of leisure pursuits to persons of similar specialized tastes—whether for horse races or museums—provided cities since early historical times with an attraction that was not merely supplementary to the advantages of work and trade, but that often determined the choice of residence. And, indeed, the images and reputations of cities have derived from these elements of "living" as well as from their importance as production centers.

Again we can go back to the Greeks for early systematic discussions of "leisure" embracing this large dimension of life's purposes and commitments apart from maintenance skills and needs. In *Of Time, Work and Leisure*, Sebastian de Grazia provides an excellent historical treatment through the early Christian, feudal, and industrial periods.[2] The working masses have always had some life outside of their work, and as Wilensky indicates, during the medieval period they had perhaps more "free time" than our own industrial workers.[3] However, the leisure concept has been generally associated with the upper classes. The "conspicuous consumption" of these classes, including those even in young America, is examined in the classic analysis of Thorstein Veblen.[4] The Greek concept of leisure was defined in terms of activities common to aristocrats and intellectuals— leisure was viewed as contemplation oriented to mind and art, firmly grounded on economic abundance, and passed along through families. This was in accord with the post-de Tocqueville assessment of what happened to higher values under democratized culture; in America, at least, the critics of mass culture lead off from this traditional suspicion of the working classes.

Yet the history of all industrial countries after World War I, and more especially after the tragedy of 1939–1946, has introduced new elements, forcing us to consider leisure in ways that go beyond traditional class limitations or expectations.

In both eastern and western Europe, nations that own or control their mass media and transportation had special needs for the study of changing life patterns. And in all nations, the rapid changes have raised basic issues of values, beginning with Jacques Ellul's assertion that technology has a momentum and an ideology of its own.[5] Bell and Toraine,[6] from the West, have their respective responses; the Czech Academy of Science, in its report *Civilization at the Crossroads,* notes the socialist approach to technology as an ideological force.[7]

Of similar importance to the cultural critics, policymakers, and futurists have been the national and international studies on leisure that have developed. In part these studies grew out of special issues such as Yugoslavia's planning of its Dalmation coast for controlled tourism, or its reevaluation of its houses of culture. In Romania, one of the special issues is the emerging popularity of television, already half a million viewers over the past decade in a nation of 20 million; in its mountains I recently observed shepherds listening to transistor radios as they watched their flock.

Led by Dumazedier, a series of important studies emerged in France, a nation which by law provides a month's vacation. In West Germany, Erwin Scheuch worked in conceptualizing a 12-nation time/money budget study,[8] while Professor Alphonse Silbermann and many others have contributed to studies in communications, community, and a wide range of issues.[9]

In other areas—the USSR, Japan, the United States, Scandinavia, England—there has developed cross-cultural cooperation of a kind that can perhaps be found in no other field as much as in these studies of leisure.

In the face of this contemporary burst of activity, no one can represent all the intellectual and research currents. What follows is, therefore, a personal view that is not insensitive to the contributions of those in many nations.

At least five basic statements can be made about leisure in all industrial societies; these will serve as a foundation for examining subsequent implications about city life.

1. Both in quality of time away from work and in the aspirations for more such free time (as seen in movement toward a five- or a four-day week), leisure has become a more positive and less peripheral value. Hence, we can now treat leisure conceptually as a social institution, on the same level as education, religion, marriage, economics, and family life. It has its characteristic social roles, values, and norms.

2. Leisure has become a major social factor, changing the familiar class categories which were based on income or type of work.

3. Contemporary workers approach leisure in the sense of holiday, not holy day, and are free of guilt. A new cosmology is decreed by the car, the television, and the credit card; heaven is at hand with a signature, without the long wait and the clean life leading eventually to an uncertain heaven.

4. The restructuring of work (utilizing flexitime, sabbaticals, and earlier retirement) provides bulk discretionary time, rather than fragmentary or disjointed time. It is this bulk time—whole days, weeks, months, or even years—that permits extended personal programming.

5. Inflation, with which we are all currently familiar, makes the dollar, the franc, the mark, or the yen worth increasingly less in exchange for goods or services; but the same complexity of socio-technological forces opens the potentials of the *hour*, or the *year*, to a new and formerly undreamed-of range of experiences.

As futurists we may assume that these tendencies for both work and leisure will continue in their basic thrust—modified work and amplified leisure. We may assume, second, not only that dramatic social change has occurred in recent decades that is qualitatively significant—such as cybernation—but also that change itself has become a social value and an expectation. That is, new leisure patterns, or at least fashions, will be accepted precisely because they are different from the past. Thus, we may assume that our social science knowledge makes it more possible to contribute to the changes taking place.

In the model which I use for the general analysis of leisure, one set of components refers to types of social orders; I call these "Conquest," "Kilowatt," "Cogno," and "Cultivated." In visual form, the hypothesis appears:[10]

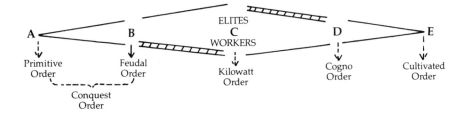

In the beginning, in the model of primitive, rural, simple society, we have a general fusion of work and leisure, so that art is part of warfare, as dance is part of religion. This convergence is destroyed as specialists (particularly as workers and elites) emerge, a distinction well developed in B, the feudal society; in the height of C, the industrial model, we even have special expenditures for play, special clothes, special times, special places, special leadership, special literature, and so on into mass media, travel, friendships, and lifestyles. Between C and D we arrive at the Cogno society, one that is conscious of its need for mature discussion of its goals and identity—the stage at which I interpret the United States to be; it is a stage of transition, not clear in either its antecedents or its desirable roads. A transitional stage is always complex, and it requires that the philosophers and the policymakers draw upon desirable elements from past models as well as from the present—strengths, for example, such as the accessibility which our popular culture provides to its masses for humanistic knowledge and for growth as well as for comfort and efficiency.

But whereas around B and C there have been sharp lines of work and nonwork, now we are less sure: The elites of mind and of management work harder while the new leisure class of workers raises its time aspirations. And what seems to be developing is again a convergence, a neo-primitive fusion. Elements of leisure, such as some I named earlier—pleasant expectation or self-growth—become ideals in the work situation; meanwhile, elements of work—such as fulfillment of oneself, discipline, and craft—find their way into leisure.

What are some implications when we find this tendency? First, the convergence of work and leisure, for all age groups, is part of other patterns which are likewise coming together. Consider such concepts as indoor–outdoor, near–far, domestic–international, urban–rural, automobile–home, and male–female.

If we apply this hypothesis to the city, four types of analysis suggest themselves: (1) the city itself as an instrument or *condition* for the new leisure–work relationship; (2) the city as a parameter for the *selection* of work–nonwork experiences; (3) the city as a functional *link* between the most localized experience and the outer world; and (4) the city in its fullest dimensions as a *meaning* about the traditional and the innovative.

The city itself as a condition for leisure and work is both a physical and an organizational unit. All of us are familiar with the dominant elements that commonly identify cities as primarily serving as locations for business, industry, education, government, play, or (as in the case of many suburbs) family residence. One or another image comes to mind with the names of Oxford, Miami Beach, Bonn, or Essen. Each image encompasses characteristic inhabitants, values, architecture, and general spirit. These are relatively small communities, and they will probably remain what they were intended to be. The changes of the future will more likely take place in larger communities and especially in the magnified community that Jean Gottmann calls the "Megalopolitan" region.[11] As in the case he studied—the 30 million persons occupying an area from Boston south to Washington, D.C.—such a super-community unifies many cities and semi-urban and rural entities into a mass of humanity and nature in which there are common values and historical traditions. In that northeastern and eastern part of the United States are to be found at one time not only the leading intellectual and cultural currents but also an area of woodland for recreational purposes that has actually expanded in the past century. The demand for parks will increase; in the past 40 years, the Commonwealth of Massachusetts has created 26 state parks of over 1,000 acres each. If we look at such megalopolitan areas as between Chicago and Milwaukee or surrounding Los Angeles, in each case the major leisure asset is the interplay of rural and urban facilities and lifestyles. Access to work in each area is similarly affected by rapid transportation by car or by the public carriers that are much discussed among us for the future.

Changing work patterns, especially in the greater use of cybernation, may affect individual cities, as in the decentralization of work. A greater impact, clearly revealed in our 1970 census, is the growth of suburbs, providing a synthesis of city and country opportunities.

The individual large city, whether or not affected by megalopolitan or region development, has greatly enlarged its range of leisure selections. The convergence of which the hypothesis speaks is, in this sense, a rebalancing of work and nonwork alternatives. My state of Florida is an unusual case in that the state population of 8.5 million places primary value on such hedonistic assets as sunshine and water, and the work that occupies many is to cater to the over 25 million tourists who now come every year. The issue there, in respect to quality of life, is how to enjoy its natural advantages without guilt (not a difficult task) and simultaneously how to enlarge those alternatives which we traditionally associate with work: finding personal dignity through being useful, establishing creative roles in retirement, and enriching leisure by such means as adult education and access to the arts.

Historically, the city has always been attractive for leisure purposes through its variety of persons, its range of potential experiences, and its possibility for excitement. The variety of persons, diversified in terms of ages, races, religions, tastes, educational backgrounds, and values, stems naturally from the variety of work. Yet an interesting phenomenon of our times is the attraction of both urban and rural areas to the youth of many countries. I had occasion recently to be in the Rocky Mountain area of Colorado, where many young people can be found living, attracted by nature as a reality and as a symbolic rejection of urbanism, work, and materialistic values. Yet in such youth magnets as Amsterdam, they continue to come for peer support, for "happenings," for curiosity, and even for interspersings of prayer and music. Youth of our time seem to be seeking this convergence of playing and praying, of work and leisure values, of stability among themselves and of restlessness among the world of others.

At least in capitalist economies, urban facilities for leisure will increase under public, semi-public, and commercial sponsorships, and my projection for the next several decades is for innovative synthesis and cross-fertilization of public and private facilities on the one hand, and for greater inclusion of leisure elements (such as libraries) within the work situation on the other hand.

I have already noted the importance of transportation within the megalopolitan context for the convergence of work and leisure. However, it is the mass media, especially television, that now provide an ongoing connection between communities of the world. Two of the classics on leisure which focus specifically on communities' patterns dealt with Middletown (Muncie, Indiana)[12] and Westchester (just north of New York City).[13] Television came after these excellent studies, and has, therefore, relegated both to history. Indeed, it is now impossible to study the leisure of any city in the Western world without relating it to the rest of the world with respect to the images it receives or sends, usually through the air.

The increase in television viewing goes far to delineate the revolution in our nonwork behavior; its effect has included the shortening or elimination of the long mid-day break from work in parts of Europe so that employees would have time for evening television entertainment. This type of demand will increase, with further modifications of work structure.

Finally, the quality of life for those in cities takes its central focus from this duality of maintenance and play in all of its variety. Lewis Mumford sees the city as a scene of human drama:

> The final mission of the city is to further man's conscious participation in the cosmic and the historic process . . . the city vastly augments man's ability to interpret these processes and take an active, formative part in them, so that every phase of the drama it stages shall have, to the highest degree possible, the illumination of consciousness, the stamp of purpose, the color of love. . . .[14]

If futurology has any obligation to help establish goals, it need go no further than Mumford, who brings to his analysis an understanding of the past as well as this ideal. In *The Future of the Future*, John McHale speaks of the need for a new city where people "may go to experiment *socially*, to explore different lifestyles, different kinds of social relationships, various tempos of living, and the possibilities of many innovative life strategies. . . ."[15] I agree with McHale, and note that the revolution in leisure as behavior and as aspiration has need for both analysis and philosophy. Philosophy cannot ignore this new development, nor can futurology and planning lose sight of philosophy.

CHAPTER 9

The Implications of Leisure Theory for Gerontology

Various segments of the population create special issues for students or decision makers in leisure. One could point to youth, to middle-aged women, to businesspersons, or to other occupational segments (especially persons in the professions, and even then to such subdivisions as teachers and medical personnel). Certainly, the elderly are a major group, affected by special attitudes held about them as well as by their relation to the economy and—increasingly—to political policy.

If we define the elderly as those over 60, there are 28 million of them in the United States. About 60 percent of the total are in good physical shape and can do what they want, within reason; 60 percent are not working. Gallup's polls reveal that about the same percentage are willing to volunteer in some community activity, but are rarely called upon. The large majority of the elderly do not live in institutions, but in some family situation or alone. Increasing numbers find their way amidst their peers, in such planned communities as Sun City Center in Florida or Leisure World in California, where they find a variety of organized activities. As one survey notes, the "little old ladies" are not rocking on the porch, but are more likely to be on the golf course, in the swimming pool, trumping their partner's aces, planning the next party, or participating in club activities.[1] Many American cities have special programs for the elderly, provided by tax-supported community centers, "Senior Citizens" or "Golden Age" clubs, or the numerous nursing homes run by churches, unions, professional organizations, and entrepreneurs.[2]

Overall, the leisure patterns of the elderly have been less studied than their problems of health, income, and housing. It seems apparent that basically the elderly can participate in the full range of alternatives open to all ages, influenced—as is everyone in her/his own situation—by income, background, and the like. Instead of the familiar practice among policy makers in the past to view the unique situation of the elderly as an accumulation of disadvantages, the trend now is to build services for and with the elderly on the basis of accumulated advantages, such as their wide experience and freedom from responsibilities.

Historically, the uniqueness of the elderly *vis-a-vis* leisure is that they have experienced more directly the dramatic changes of the past half century—the loosening of social class restrictions, the release from a work ethic, large internal migrations, the spread of art and literacy, the growth of public services, and the companionship-oriented family; they have lived through major wars, a great Depression, rising costs, and the birth of cars, planes, television, and astronauts. Having lived at a time when many of them carried water from the well, they now see a life in which the middle-class home is filled with mechanical "servants."

It is clear that a theory of leisure for any one age or social segment must fall within a larger theory of leisure. That theory, in turn, must account for those objective or subjective factors that enter into the meaning of the lifespan. Yet beyond this, such an encompassing theory of leisure must attempt to combine the microcosmic and macrocosmic levels or ranges, to permit an analysis of a single, relatively isolated, and complete experience, such as a game, as well as of its relationships to the largest ideology and historical era. Thus, we need a map of leisure elements which is always larger than the immediate need and which lends itself to empirical research as well as to *verstehen* social science, philosophical and humanistic judgments, and policy formation. I shall not insist that one model can fulfill these specifications, but with advancing years I am courageous enough to have developed one on the gratuitous assumption that the new generation of scholars may at least learn by the process of criticism. Since this model has already been presented, I can turn to some implications for gerontology of each component from its first level—*conditions, selections, dynamics,* and *meanings.*

The objective *conditions* of leisure—for all social groups—include time, age, work role, health, income, residential location, and family situation. For retired persons we can enumerate several specific factors:

1. The time at their disposal is *continuous* or *bulk* time, not—as in the work life—fragmentary time. For example, the hours from 9 A.M. to 5 P.M., on a five-day count, and from the ages of 60 to 75 come to a total of over 31,000 hours. It is also true for the elderly, as we have noted for other segments of the population, that as the value of the dollar has gone *down,* the potential of the hour for older persons in their total leisure has gone *up.* Indeed, all economic considerations of increases in time are far greater

than the mere statistics show if this increase is noted—in access to people and places through travel, to literacy, and to the world itself through the mass media.

Thus, we have a major new element in leisure experiences that requires relatively continuous periods of attention, such as travel, study, or voluntary activities which require going to other neighborhoods, communities, or even nations.

2. Economic inflation over many years and our relatively less developed welfare plans mean that the elderly are often poor—with one of every four below the poverty level. This factor often operates as a deterrent in utilization of the new increment of bulk time, especially as it relates to the costs of travel.

3. The loss of the full-time production role is, of course, the crucial condition of the new leisure, for it raises such questions as the ongoing usefulness of values from the work life—a situation especially critical for the person who retires from business. Therefore, in many industrial nations the nature of pre-retirement education is increasingly re-formulated as a preparation which is ideally built into the humanistic development from childhood onward. For many persons who have refused to consider the reality of retirement or of aging, this transition to a role of economic uselessness in the urban setting may come suddenly and traumatically. Leisure in this sense serves as an instrumental bridge, one of its conceptions noted earlier.

4. In many societies, certainly in a dynamic, youth-and action-oriented one such as the United States, rejection of or indifference toward the elderly creates an important question: Can the content of leisure itself provide a lifestyle of sufficient meaning to replace the contribution of work to one's identity and self-worth? This issue grows in its qualitative dimension if we take Dr. Alex Comfort and other geriatricians at their word when they say that the aging process can be slowed down enough to keep us alive another 20 years by the end of the century.

Finally, the vast change into an industrial society, and now into a cybernated or post-industrial society, has produced a generation of elderly pioneers who in many cases have gone from peasant villages to lifestyles of the jet-age.

When we turn to the second major element of the model—the *selection* of leisure activities and experiences by the elderly—these several conditions interweave. For example, the attitude toward aging by the general public is strongly influenced by the geriatric, biological model of life as one of accumulative incapacity; i.e., as older persons become slower, they are less able to learn. The familiar disengagement theory moves in that direction. It is true that many older persons *are* less active, they *do* withdraw, they *do* drop out, they *do* lose purpose. For instance, we have 80,000 retired military personnel in or near Tampa–St. Petersburg, Florida; in our studies of them we discover alienation, alcoholism, short-term illusory golf as life's content, and perhaps more suicides than the public knows. Yet it is dangerous to assume that older persons can do only what they are doing now. They often do what they are permitted to do by a self-image perpetuated by the society.[3] Many surveys of their retirement activities are therefore misleading, feeding this tautology.

If, on the other hand, psychology and other social sciences utilize Maslow and Erikson in this matter, the assumption is that *every* age has its limits and its strengths; the purpose of research then is *to measure not only the reality but also the creative possibility*. This cannot be done by hypothetical questions of the what-would-you-like-to-do sort. It can be observed best in the simulation, the demonstration, the observation of older persons in natural conditions, outside of the academic laboratory. For instance, at Boston University, in 1961–62, we had 45 older persons studying piano or painting over an 18-month period, taught by young students. This tested our hypothesis that leisure, especially through the arts, can be future-oriented, providing new purpose and, indeed, new life for the elderly.

It is apparent that many older persons throughout the world are defying the popular industrial image that they are increasingly useless: throughout the United States they are to be found in adult education courses; at New York University and now at Case-Western Reserve in Cleveland there are special programs for retirees with sufficient backgrounds; in Winnetka, near Chicago, the creativity of older persons is illustrated as they serve as tutors to school children; Little House of Menlo Park, California, is among the best known of several thousand active centers in which older persons can be observed daily in political discussions, in libraries, in preparation for volunteer activities, or in rehearsal for theatrical performances. Except for the realization that a 70-year-old usually does not play tennis all afternoon or run foot races, we become increasingly aware that the attitude and pattern of the culture more than the biology of the situation shape our expectations and fulfillments in leisure.

This conclusion opens the range of possibilities, but it also reminds us that older persons share in their cultures. If *they* believe themselves to be incapable of new experiences, or to be unwise in deviating from the familiar patterns of their friends, then a large range of theoretical issues emerges for program builders: How wise is it to seek new patterns for leisure of the elderly? Do some types of leisure actions develop more easily than others— for instance, travel to new places rather than participation in new clubs? More difficult yet is whether, following the "humanistic coefficient" of

Znaniecki's sociology (which underlies my construct of leisure), we can impose our values upon the established values of other persons.[4] It is an ethical problem, and suggests that we should seek to expose other persons to a broad range of challenges and help to develop their own security in rejecting as well as in accepting. *The criterion of success then is the exposure which has been provided under excellent leadership, rather than the conversion of the behavior.*

Another consequence of this approach is that the leader of leisure activities must be convinced that there is no abstract or absolute hierarchy of leisure values, but that within a general situation there are opportunities for expansion or growth which may be creatively developed. For example, about 60 miles from my home is the Disney World—its technological, passive, and highly organized program attracts over 10 million Americans every year; a few miles farther down the crowded highway is a once-quiet community called Orlando, where there is a new library, a lovely lake, and an excellent symphony orchestra of retirees. Not only are all of these alternatives available with the new time, but also each has its own valid meanings, whether adventure, curiosity, educational growth, enjoyment of nature, or creative expression. It is the purpose of the leisure leader to respect each function as a beginning and then seek to enrich its content. A simple illustration of this possibility is the Greater Boston Youth Symphony Orchestra, for whose beginnings I had some responsibility, and which increased in importance to its young members as it played more challenging music with ever high standards of quality.

The dynamic of the selection process is the interaction which takes place among the external conditions, the internal taste or "personality" in the broad sense, and such personal mediating factors as the nature of one's family, the weather, a newspaper story, or an unusual television show. Seldom does one factor determine the selection; the leader is, therefore, only one intervening factor, and she/he must always be sensitive to the full situation.

As to functions, leisure serves the person in ways that, on the one hand, are obvious, observable, or *manifest.* For example, if passing the time quickly is itself important, some experiences are more effective than others. Some experiences succeed, as intended, in bringing one together with friends or in avoiding loneliness and boredom. Some, again, such as reading or writing a book require effort and may produce intellectual growth, personal satisfactions, social status, or an influence on others. These kinds of functions, which largely occupy the literature, can to some degree be weighted, measured, or predicted.

There are, however, other functions of leisure which are more subtle, informal, and difficult to attach to a specific action or span of time. These *latent* functions, I suggest, take us away from an unfortunate association of leisure with activity, and enable us to deal with deeper socio-psychological levels of symbolic behavior. The clue, I propose, lies in a series of dialectic processes; these, in their total scope, lend to leisure the ultimate distinction from religious, educational, or work institutions. Among the dichotomies or poles of the dialectic through which activities and experiences may be analyzed are movement and rest, freedom and discipline, play and entertainment, sociability and isolation, construction and distraction, self-growth and recreation, self-worth and self-defeat. Permit me here to consider just the first set—movement and rest—because it is a polarity of great importance to the elderly.

One effect of industrialization is that the aging process is less related to a characteristic progression from restlessness to rest; modern transportation has supplied the potential of physical movement, and the mass media have produced magical changes. In pre-technological cultures there is a sharp distinction between going to the world and bringing the world to us. But in our current culture, television provides the viewer with the simultaneous possibilities of being at rest and in movement. For this reason I was not too surprised to learn in Bucharest in 1971 that the Romanian TV shows most popular among its half million viewers were those dealing with space science. For, of course, there are several kinds of limited physical movement. There is, first, movement in the home, not so much with respect to intensive physical expenditure as to the relation of architecture to patterns of leisure use and, incidentally, of movement. Indeed, the larger issue of space enters here because mechanical energy can transport man to larger spaces in shorter time. In the home, however, space is more a matter of arrangement in efficiency and comfort than in the preservation of physical energy. The new leisure has led to a new architecture, implying such items as "family" rooms, "Florida" rooms, basement "recreation" rooms, television rooms, and so on.

There can be little doubt that travel will continue to increase among the elderly; economic condition, not lack of courage or interest, will serve as the main barrier. Age breakdowns in various studies of tourism confirm this trend.

As to the concept of "rest," there are 14 defintions in Webster's *New World Dictionary* (1960). All point to a general state of immobility: peace, ease, and refreshment as produced by sleep; refreshing ease or inactivity after work or exertion; relief from anything distressing. It is common, especially in institutional settings, to see older persons—and not always the oldest—adopt rest as a new lifestyle; they simply sit or lie, day upon day. In Florida, with the provision several years ago of federal aid for older persons, many nursing homes have been created as profit-making businesses in which the collective television set may be the major investment for recreational purposes. Yet it is apparent that people are sensitive to the contagion of group atmosphere. Considering the element of creativity, I have seen a home for the elderly transformed from a pre-grave atmosphere by an energetic young lady who involved its residents in repairing furniture, painting pictures for the rooms and halls, and developing a weekly newsletter. She found ways of involving even bed-ridden residents by having them discover ways of creative participation, as in selecting wallpaper.

The contemporary view of leisure must include its usefulness as a tool in mental and emotional therapy. As in the case of art as therapy, I am aware of the purists who throw up their hands at any association of these terms; but as with art, leisure is *involvement* or action which can include the restorative function; on the priority scale of the participant—at a given moment of the day or of her/his life—this may be its chief value.

In summary, the leaders and planners of leisure experiences for the elderly can view the continuum of movement–rest as one dimension of the dynamic at their disposal, seeking for all ages a sensitive balance or emphasis as warranted by the situation. Finally, it would be possible and intriguing to arrive at various concrete programs in a community center, not by thinking at all of activities—games, art, sociability, etc.—but by starting with such dynamic polarizations or processes as freedom–discipline, play–entertainment, or self-growth–recreation. We might then go from concepts of function which are relevant to certain situations, groups, or persons to the invention of activities and experiences that are presently blocked out by traditional categories.

The same dynamic approach can be illustrated in the difficult area of the *meanings* of leisure for the elderly. We could follow classifications which fall into apparently neat psychological boxes: something is "liked" or "enjoyed," it "brings back memories," it "makes me happier," and so on. All of these are legitimate types of meanings, for when they are given, it is hardly necessary to push the subject further. If the person is pushed about what she/he means by "liking," she/he will inevitably come to similar terms which will be equally subjective. This direct approach of asking people what a given leisure activity or experience means to them will always remain useful, although it is limited by the subject's sensitivity, frankness, and self-knowledge and by her/his level of articulation and rapport with the questioner.

A second approach to meanings is for the scientist to work with models of lifestyles and personalities. Ruth Benedict's division of whole tribes into Dionysian and Apollonian is well known.[5] The pioneering work in social psychology, Thomas and Znaniecki's *Polish Peasant*, introduced a trinity of personality types: Philistine, Bohemian, and Creative[6]; a more contemporary scheme is David Riesman's Inner-directed, Other-directed, and Autonomous.[7] Familiar in the vernacular are the "introvertive" and "extrovertive" types that were systematically explored by Adler and others. In each case, what we have is a set of characterizations that are constructed from a series of behaviors, and, therefore, provide some predictive possibilities for future behavior and attitudes. A simple example of this approach is seen when a leader of recreational activities identifies one person as "active," another as "passive." In deciding where we are dispensable or most useful, we all prescribe somewhat to this tradition of putting persons into groups. Our own motivations and policies on this matter need ongoing re-examination, especially with respect to our own images and stereotypes.

A third approach to leisure meanings that is especially applicable to the elderly deals with symbols. I need hardly do more than remind ourselves of the close identity of leisure with social symbols—with the feeling of being an elite of the society, a member of a class or a subculture such as youth; leisure has relationships to religious and family symbols, to occupational legends and mythologies, to notions of eschatology, to birth and rebirth. Freud and Veblen have provided insights on general levels, and Huizinga's analysis of games has supplied clues for a lifetime of study. In the American literature I recommend the writings of Kenneth Burke and his protege Hugh Duncan whose insights are yet to be adequately applied to the leisure field.[8]

An inescapable fact is that the older person has traditionally served as a symbol of the past to younger generations. The young, often impatient with the past, reject its living representatives. Yet technology, urbanization, and the growing freedom of personal action combine to diminish age as the crucial factor in social organization. With a move toward earlier retirement everywhere, the leisure patterns of older persons would appear to open new opportunities for breaking the correlation of aging with either passivity or history. One conclusion, if this trend of thought were to be extended, is that there is a need for inventing and encouraging leisure programs in which several generations are quite naturally brought together in experiences that go beyond age or physical capacity, and, particularly, that can draw upon the past, present, and future orientations. This, however, takes us into a fourth dimension in analyzing the meanings of leisure.

The epistomological approach to leisure, as I use the phrase, refers to a threefold view of man's relationship to the world, which has been presented in Chapter 4:

1. An *assumptive* relationship based on knowledge and sentiments that reach into the past, resting on belief, affirmation, legend, and folklore;

2. An *analytic* relationship based on an attempt to understand, question, and experiment;

3. An *aesthetic* or *transformative* relationship based on creative action and directed toward the future, resting on the reordering of ideas, objects, social institutions, and organizations.

These approaches, in short, permit us to *live* in the world, *understand* it, or *change* it. Of course, these overlap, even if they are illustrated by such clear entities as religion, science, and art. Each, nevertheless, provides motivation and character for some leisure activities and experiences.

The assumptive type of relatedness applies whenever we engage in an activity which is a complete statement, such as playing a game, fishing, taking a trip, watching television, reading a book, visiting a friend—the list is infinite. No explanation is needed, no further rationale; the activity speaks for itself. Why are you reading a book? Why are you visiting a friend? These are unnecessary questions, even though *this* book, or *this* friend, is not worth much. Each page read, each visit made, each fish caught by an individual verifies a pattern long ingrained and accepted. No bravery is required; no individuality is asserted. It is an immersion in the world *as it is.*

When, however, we turn to analytic illustrations of leisure, we enter a potentially more upsetting enterprise, both to the society and to the person. Here, we have the general momentum of the reading, as an example, and the issue becomes the *content* of the reading. If we turn to our television for a special program on the population explosion, the simple item, "watching television," becomes a far deeper matter of potential social change.

It would seem that the aesthetic approach turns us naturally to art as the content of leisure—art either as a creative act or as a set of ex-periences to enjoy. And this is true in part. Yet the core of the aesthetic is not art works but the process of creating. But is creativity limited to painting pictures? Maslow speaks of creativity in homemaking. He equates the aesthetic with the need for "self-actualization" which develops and is fulfilled only after the "lower" needs—physiological, safety, belonging, love, and esteem—are satisfied.[9] Actualization can come from transforming block dwellings into a community as well as from turning rough motifs into a musical composition.

Transformative leisure can take us from the creation of art works to membership in a community effort for eradicating crime. For example, several hundred older persons, including those without professional qualifications, came to speak for their generation at the 1971 White House Conference held in Washington, D.C., devoting themselves with the rest of us to changing the society. Also, the struggle of our black population to achieve equality provides a dramatic instance of the transformative use of time by persons of all ages.

These examples raise a question as to whether the hypothesis would stand up that older persons are necessarily engaged in leisure which points backward, where there is security and tradition. The question to be asked is whether this truism will hold as strongly in the several decades ahead. With the growth of mass media, travel, literacy, and political identity among this segment of the population, can we envision a somewhat comparable growth of courage, individuality, and adventure through new experiences which we have usually associated with younger persons? Indeed, should it be our purpose to encourage a continuum of values and meanings through leisure which will point the person toward the future as well as to the present and the past? It is a rather intriguing thought that perhaps what young people may need most is a more historical orientation, and the elderly, a more futuristic orientation. This was, in fact, a central hypothesis in our Boston program in the arts for persons over 65; with the arts, they consciously and subconsciously were dealing with the future of materials and of themselves; in the same project, their teachers were all college students who profited from this intimate contact with representatives of the past.

The ideal model for elderly persons—perhaps for all ages—provides some balance between leisure and large life patterns which draw actively upon past, present, and future directions. One simple example which, in fact, combines all three and yet draws clear lines is a project in which young people and elderly relatives or strangers sit together before a tape recorder to discuss both memories of their past—each probing the other—and their respective analyses of the current changes and their hopes for the future. In one such project some years ago in the low mountains above New York City, the youth group dramatized the history of the area in the form of a pageant, and then invited the older group to see and respond to the depiction.

Several broad observations, aimed toward the future, will now take us beyond the four components of our model.

1. *Chronological or biological age will decline as a major variable in social relationships, although it will never disappear.*

Age is only one of the variables that enter into the objective conditions that shape the selection of leisure. Others are time (in its quantity and its structure), health, income, education, place of residence, work background, and character or "personality." As access to distant places is increased through easier transportation, or as images of the world are more plentiful through communications, biological age barriers give way. Tourist agencies can substantiate their increasing dependence on older travelers in off-season tours, and the television industry will someday wake up to the huge, faithful audience which presently it ignores.

Biological age becomes a declining variable as a social gerontology develops in the United States, as already it is developing in France. For the new philosophical and scientific basis for social gerontology leaves the geriatric model and turns to the accumulative experiences of older age as a strategic strength. Erik Erikson and Abe Maslow are among those who have shown how to develop human inventories based on potential growth and limitations of every age, as more recently Simone de Beauvoir has provided a positive statement of aging itself.[10] As the French authoress seeks to break what she calls the "conspiracy of silence"—that is, the treatment of the elderly as nonpersons—what she is properly doing is removing the negativism of our culture toward aging, and simultaneously reducing its importance as a factor in the policy of the leisure professions. In those experiments where persons of various generations have been brought together for in-depth discussions, there develop techniques for more potential interaction. The members of a symphony orchestra in Florida in which I have played range in age from 15 to 75; and someday we may see major universities where classes will have as many students in their 60's as in their 20's.

2. *Increasingly, during the half-century span from one's 20th to one's 70th year, the person will decide how "old" she/he wants to be with respect to lifestyle.*

   As a teacher for some 30 years, I suggest that there are students who at the age of 20 have chosen to die intellectually; on the other hand, and as the years have gone by, larger numbers of the middle-aged and elderly attend our classes or take more active roles in the community. Cases of voluntary disengagement among the elderly are balanced by those of voluntary engagement in community programs such as SCORE. The recent growth of 3,000 or 4,000 communes in the United States, with an average life span of three to four years, is an attempt by young people to participate in a pre-launderette, pre-electronic, pre-industrial mode of life which is a negation of the activism often associated in the symbols of our society with youth.

   Indeed, it is this symbolic dimension that will be of special interest in the "turquoise" model of which Johnston writes—one that falls between the fully work-oriented and the Utopian leisure-oriented models.[11] Recall that both work and leisure have provided powerful symbols on the levels of social class and of age. Recall also that presently in the United States the common symbolic association—with some factual justification—is of elderly and poor. A third symbolic component provides the formula: old–poor–inactive.

   The productive level of today already makes possible the elimination of poverty among all persons, young or old, black or white. It is a political problem, not an economic one—one of priorities, not resources. And increasingly, therefore, as we look several decades ahead, the political process will be based on moral issues. That is one consequence of a society of abundance. That may, frankly, be an expression of hope more than of fact, and yet the present revolutions among the youth, the women, the blacks, the church congregants, and the environmentalists (who come from all populations) give credance to this forecast.

   Thus, secondly, I submit that the reduction of poverty and of biological age limitations opens the door to a freer choice of lifestyles, whether symbolized by degrees of activity, by leisure actions, or by an internal and psychological security.

I need hardly add that this new possibility—the* choice of one's psychological and lifestyle age—will lead to new issues for counselling, research, and policy.

3. *As we have left the productivity or work domination of the industrial or Kilowatt society and become immersed for the past quarter of a century in a self-critical mood of the Cogno society, new perceptions of time will affect the choices we make in lifestyles.*

The clock, as Woodcock noted, was a major symbol of industrial society.[12] It still remains a possession of the majority of older persons by force of habit, or by the need to structure one's time around pills or Lawrence Welk. I currently have a student who is asking people in the Williams Park of St. Petersburg what time it is; he then records how many have watches and how far they are in error if they have to surmise the time. Comparisons are being made with young people. He finds that 85 percent of older males have watches, compared to 48 percent of males in their 20's. Fifty-two percent of older women have watches, but only 39 percent of young females. When it comes to guessing the time without watches, young girls are wrong by an average span of 47.04 minutes; older women were wrong by less than 27 minutes.

Time, wrote the philosopher Kant, "is not an independent substance nor an objective determination of things . . . but the form of inner sense, that is, of the perception of ourselves and our inner state. . . ."[13] A new set of issues is emerging when the constants of this "form of inner sense" are less constant. Work is one such constant; the television program is another form of constant. There is also a relation of time to type of activity. We know, for example, that a more complex activity requires more attention, is usually more interesting, and causes time to seem to go more quickly than a simple activity. Boredom, in reverse, emerges from the dearth of anything absorbing. On the perspective of weeks, months, and years, we react to rhythms of events and create rituals and ceremonies to mark time periods.

Too little inquiry has been made by contemporary social scientists regarding the translation of temporal rhythms and discontinuities into the lives of individuals and families or into the changes in traditions of subcultures, communities, and whole cultures. On the national level, the Communists tried to do away with the sacred connotations of the week, whether the holy day was Sunday for Christians, Saturday for Jews, or Friday for Moslems. As Wilbert Moore[14] notes, in 1929 the USSR turned to a continuous work week, with one day in five (but not the same day for all workers) taken off for rest. Chaos resulted. Two years of this, and in 1931 a six-day week was started, with the same off-day for all. In 1940 the Russians returned to the familiar seven-day week, including Sunday as the common day of rest. One gets a feel for some of the semantic antics that can result by reading a government edict in Prague:

> Because Christmas Eve falls on a Thursday, the day has been designated a Saturday for work purposes. Factories will close all day, with stores open a half day only. Friday, December 25, has been designated a Sunday, with both factories and stores open all day. Monday, December 28, will be a Wednesday for work purposes. Wednesday, December 30, will be a business Friday. Saturday, January 2, will be a Sunday, and Sunday, January 3, will be a Monday.

One issue for the elderly is that under the tradition of full retirement, they confront a bulk of enormous potential emptiness. Some of those who are now being observed in Williams Park by my student will, with or without a watch, sit in the park for about 15 years, eight hours a day, most days of the week, for a total of over 30,000 hours. If in the decades ahead it develops that many persons will have to choose from among various time plans for work and nonwork, what perceptions will they bring to the decision? And how will these perceptions be correlated with the age variable?

Already it is clear that as inflation makes the dollar less useful, technology makes the hour more useful. With the dollar we can do less, as all the elderly who live on savings know; with the hour we now have larger potentials for experience. The "trade-off" of time for income will be influenced by this imbalance, and it cries now for a new social science attempt to create models of time perception. With respect to this problem we are perhaps where psychology was before Freud. Gerontology would seem to offer one potential home base for such research.

4. *The flexibility of work life will be aided by lifetime work and nonwork plans and contracts.*

The guaranteed annual income, in one form or another, will have become an academic matter by the end of the century, as I see the trend. It should be relatively simple to establish hour "banks," and to permit the borrowing of bulk periods of time for travel, education, or any other private purpose with the same kind of collateral on which we now borrow money. It may not be unusual, some decades from now, to find a 65-year-old working to pay back the hours borrowed when she/he was 45.

New combinations of labor, management, and government will develop, in response to cybernation and to aspirations of everyone for time. Juanita Kreps has spelled out in considerable detail several alternatives for new economic arrangements, including retirement at age 38.[15] Phillip Bosserman has proposed other work and nonwork options, based on daily, weekly, monthly, and yearly frameworks.[16] To management consultant Miller Faught, "Thank God, it's Wednesday," should become a common sigh in closing the shortened work week. One possibility presented by the United States at an international conference on architecture and recreation is this:

> One work shift would be on duty 10 hours per day, from Monday to Wednesday—a 30-hour work week—and have the next four days off—a 4-day weekend. The other shift would work Thursday through Saturday—a 30-hour work week also—and have the next four days off. Sunday would be common to all these new 4-day weekends, but the longer recreation period would presumably level out the stress made on our recreation facilities. Fewer people would arrive at the same places at the same times because more people would have time to go farther from home to other recreation areas and have time to construct a counter-peak time visit of their own choosing.[17]

If we reconsider these four broad trends, direct implications for the elderly are clear:

1. If biological age diminishes as a variable in social organization, the elderly are free to more openly engage in any and all leisure activities. The only limits are physical, not psychological.

2. If an adult of any biological age can have greater choice of lifestyle—i.e., freedom to decide to be as old or as young as she/he desires—we may anticipate a freer mixture of generations in their leisure, and a new sense of exploration or innovation among the elderly.

3. If new time perceptions emerge, we may find more ongoing leisure programs for the elderly, especially in the arts, education, and community service.

4. If there develops a variety of work patterns within a variety of time structures, we may expect similar varieties of leisure patterns which become dominant goals, with work plans chosen as instrumental means for more effective leisure. The "energy crisis" will further this tendency.

These, then, are a few of the trends which I call the "neo-primitive." The primitive social order is fundamentally one where such institutions or patterns as play, art, work, religion, government, and tribe are not as specialized in terms of role or structure as ours. The fusions of today and tomorrow have a strong material base, a technological energy system, transportation and communications miracles, and an urban complexity. Further, post-primitive individuals, both in the Orient and the Occident, both in the socialist and the nonsocialist societies, are raising these questions of goals. And the questions are not inhibited by academic, discipline-oriented frameworks, but are open, cross-disciplinary, and cross-national, and go to the heart of man's condition. As the issue was put in *Civilization at the Crossroads* by a joint team of the Czechoslovak Academy of Science:

> From work, through education, consumption and leisure there is a wide range of big and small opportunities to promote technical, scientific, social or simply human creativeness. The time will certainly come when the traditional dominants of life prove inadequate. Here and now we should be thinking about new functions of factories, schools, mass communication and entertainment facilities, centres of technology, science and culture. We should consider establishing a network of institutions open to everyone who feels the need for active contact with the world of technology and innovation, with an atmosphere of developing human powers.[18]

The conclusion seems clear, to me at least, that the general trends I have summarized seem to widen "contact with the world" for the elderly of tomorrow. With biological age a lesser consideration and with selection of lifestyle more a personal decision, there will be a greater freedom and, therefore, a responsibility for the individual, with the inevitable proportion of those to whom such freedoms spell confusion and fear. But there will also be a greater prospect of "contact" for those who today are handicapped in their creative expression by attitudes about aging in the culture as a whole.

Loose references to "several decades hence" or to the "elderly of tomorrow" suggest some tightening of our time referrents. I propose that we attempt this, at least in setting the issue. What we will see as one outcome, and an overriding issue at that, is the need for new conceptualization of our central term, "leisure."

A quick historical review shows immediately the fundamental importance of what I will call the "gerontological watershed" of our century. It was the crucial 15-year period between 1932 and 1947. That 15-year period embraced three significant events: the Depression, World War II, and the launching of television. The line I would suggest is between those who were middle-aged when those major developments took place and those who were very young. On the one hand, those of us who are now in our 60's were in our teens and 20's during the period I mention; if we are now in our 70's we were in our 20's and 30's then; if we are in our 80's now, we were in our 30's at the start of the Depression and in our 40's at the advent of television.

That is to say, these people who presently comprise the bulk of those in nursing homes, or wearing Senior Power badges, or reading *Harvest Years* and *Modern Maturity,* are persons who were lucky to finish high school; who listened to Fred Allen on radio; who were largely raised in small towns without cars, phones, or refrigerators; who remember the Depression; and who saw Charlie Chaplin films the first time around. Further, among our 28 million over 60, the majority either had an immigrant mother or father or were themselves born abroad.

These, altogether, are pioneers in American retirement. If, indeed, many of them are bored, or have found difficulty in the transition to retirement, what models did they have? What social welfare leaders did they have to turn to except those like Edward Lindemann, Clark Tibbitt, and Wilma Donahue who were themselves pioneers in a young field?

In contrast are the potential retirees. Those who are today in their 20's and 30's will reach their 60's after the turn of the century, and to them the Depression is book history, while color television and walks on the moon are the reality. When they reach full retirement—if there is such a thing in 20 or 30 years, except for the incapacitated—they will have been raised in a new world, one where revolutions in values will have taken place in religious, family, and educational life, and where the majority of the elderly will have taken jumbo jets for granted, will have been raised largely in large American urban areas, and will have been exposed to considerable formal education, scientism, kitchen disposals, and computerized credit cards. The elderly of this milieu, as well as the first group I described, are the proper concern of present-day gerontology. This differential between the elderly of today and those of tomorrow tells us that realistically we must develop a new gerontology to parallel the new milieu of retirement.

CHAPTER 10

Leisure and the Design Profession

The designer has always needed to know her/his craft, whether grounded in mechanics, architecture, physics, or any other skill; this was the basic assumption of the guild system and apprenticeship. More recently, institutional training has produced designers who know more history about themselves, more theory, more about new relationships to other disciplines, more about new experiments; all this, we are all aware, is sometimes achieved at the expense of practical craft or skill.

There is little doubt that, difficult as it may be, the contemporary designer must possess the traditional know-how as well as be aware of the broad directions her/his field is taking. Yet a third demand has in recent years become evident, from such personal stimulants as Lewis Mumford, Frank Lloyd Wright, and Buckminster Fuller, and from the objective lessons and implications of social change as a whole, seen in the impact of computerization, urban renewal, new home patterns, population growth, or a hundred other evidences of a new world; it is, obviously, a new world in which science, technology, planning, and design are inevitably meshed with human or personal tendencies. This can no longer be a matter of choice by technicians—or even artists and professors—whose laboratories, studies, and classrooms are relevant it they are related.

The social or human side is not new, even in practice. As far back as the mid-1930's the physical plans for a federal village near Milwaukee— Greendale—were supposedly developed on the basis of desires and needs of potential residents as determined by questionnaires which some of us had to interpret. A homely example is the presence of the market research agency to tell the industrial designers whether the typical consumer will prefer a round or a square waffle iron. In such a case where a product has to be fitted to personality characteristics, the argument has long ago ended. For here the designer works for an industry which must sell its products, which engages the designer and, therefore, controls the situation.

The new issue goes much beyond—when there is no immediate market, when the designer is still on his own, when the fruition of design is in the future. How do you plan a school plant which, a decade from now, may become a resource center for all generations and be used simultaneously by them? Or, as put to me in London by the president of the largest combine of news publications:

> How do we design a communications system socially as well as technologically when reading is now supplemented and may be replaced by microfilm, microfiche, cable TV, cassette systems, and other gadgetry yet to come?[1]

Such issues obviously take the designer beyond professional skills, but not beyond professional commitments. For the commitments are no longer as narrow as they were before the physicists joined the moral dispute following Hiroshima. The new commitment, however, is still more intellectual on the part of the designers, or scientists as a whole, than it is emotional or visceral. This results in part from their training and in part from the types of persons attracted to these fields. For example, science, engineering, and business students are more conservative socially and politically than other students, but they also attend fewer concerts, lectures, or similar exposures to so-called humanistic or aesthetic images.

In the industrial–business complex, design was first geared to the products made for sale. Advertising at the turn of the century revolved around the virtues of the product, a general emphasis that lasted until World War II. Then, with the boom of the mass media, and especially television in the 1950's, the advertiser became a central strategist, alongside the inventor–designer and the financier–manufacturer–businessperson. This third leg of the stool, advertising, took on a double job, tapping the consumer's wants and shaping her/his needs. John Kenneth Galbraith describes this new approach in *The New Industrial State*.[2] This meant advertisers had to become social scientists as well as hucksters. To know how to shape consuming behavior, they had to learn something about consuming in relation to living. To understand who listens to what on television and what its outcomes are, you had better know something about the power structure in the family and the relationships in time between bathroom, bedroom, and kitchen and the location of the television set—something, I suspect, about which the industry knows little.

Yet the scope becomes larger, for *living* patterns, although they encompass *buying* patterns, are only a part of cultural and communication factors in the local, regional, national, international, and historical sense. Any market researcher or designer of products, buildings, or cities who has not read the writings of Fuller, the Goodmans, Jacques Ellul, Janet Jacobs, Margaret Mead, Illich, and a host of interpreters of social change is not in touch with the realities of our time.

The problem, of course, is how to isolate issues which relate design to social trends, how to proceed in analysis once the issues are identified, how to draw policy implications. These can only be touched upon through the juxtaposition of several models which will be quickly described: a model relating design as a whole to the new world: a model relating one specific trend among many—leisure—to the same new world; and, third, a proposed fusion of the two models, with some meanings for both.

A model, as I use the term, is a working map: it must seek to meet both specific and general analyses; it must be spaceless and timeless, and yet be firmly rooted in both dimensions. The model must contain components and, within each, elements that are in part measurable, structured for computer purposes, and yet stimulating to the imagination. There must be an interlocking or interfacing between the parameters or levels, and, above all, there must be a general substructure which will surround any variety of submodels or themes for analysis.

In the present case, our themes are design and leisure. Each will constitute the innermost square of a four-squared construction.

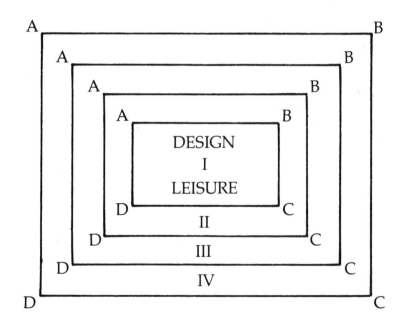

Within this broad construct, the field of design may be divided into four components—Context, Conditions, Creation, Critique—providing a total appearance of the model:

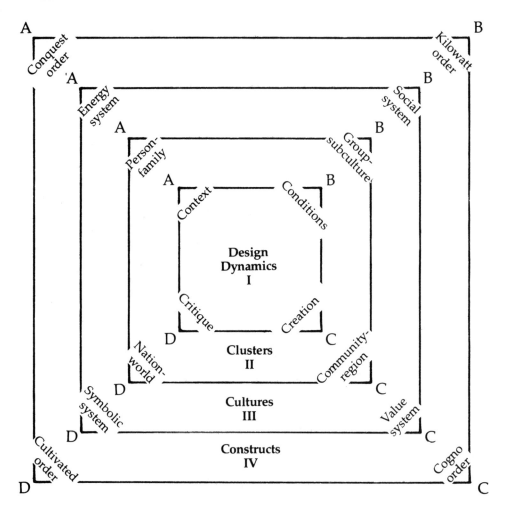

Permit me now to play with this model, drawing from its immensity only one observation relating to each component.

By *context*, I refer primarily to one's philosophy as a designer, the purpose of the particular assignment, and the motivations of the client or patron.

A central shift is taking place in all that is crucial and that holds some clues regarding both the future of the private sector and the destiny of the United States as a whole. As a highly simplified proposition: *After the attention in production and design turned from the making and selling of a product to the simultaneous creation of a potentially favorable consumer, the inevitable progression now is to the creation of a favorable environment.* Industry, capital, and business have only begun to sense this.

A polymer chemist at MIT, after doing considerable consulting for a major firm, was sent three blank checks by the firm: one to write in whatever salary he wanted, one to underwrite whatever staff he wanted, and one to pay for any equipment. However, to accept a permanent position, he would have to move to a small town in Michigan, the firm's headquarters. My friend immediately tore up the checks. He likes living in Boston too much—he liked its symphony, its beauty, its intellectual dynamic. On a national level, we see citizens from all walks of life questioning the assessment of technology in purely pragmatic terms. Fundamentally, the new concern may be summarized in the terms of *possibilities* and *values*. *Abundance—for What?* was David Riesman's question in a volume of that title. The implications of this question for designers flow from a concern with their own goals and actual power, and this is in part suggested in the second principle.

The second component of design—*condition*—includes the materials available to you, the degree of freedom and control, and the important element of time. From merely the last, I submit one observation: *The longer the planning perspective in time, the more power the design professions have over their own goals and philosophies.*

American industry is entirely committed to planning. Good planning, except in such nervous industries as television, now forces corporations to look ahead in years or even in decades as it used to in months. On the labor-management front, negotiations are increasingly based on annual periods. Since the American union movement is prepared ideologically to accept cybernation as long as workers do not suffer financially, some forms of guaranteed annual income are inevitable, and not only for the poor. My projection is that by the 1980's we will see lifetime contracts (to be discussed more fully in Chapter 11), based not on years of service but on some accumulated measurements of time, energy, or accomplishments.

Uniquely, the design component in industry is adaptable to long-range thinking because its most cherished possession is freedom, and a future-orientation is characteristically freer, influencing the present even in its statement of goals or forms for tomorrow. Here, the relationship of design and the aesthetic is evident, for the world of art illustrates a responsive and predictive possibility matched in the scientific sphere by science fiction or by the intuitive flashes among scientists which can be understood better as aesthetic processes than as analytic. (For further consideration of this, I recommend Arthur Koestler's two volumes, *The Act of Creation* and *The Sleepwalkers*.[3])

The third component of design—*creation*—comes to grips with such basic elements as engineering, aesthetic processes, intuition, and craft. It is on this level of concern that the serious designer is often most frustrated, and sees her/his power and potential hedged in by the context and conditions set out by the client. Yet, even a quick glance at the multiple variables of the construct suggests a growing complexity of influences with which the client or the corporation has to deal. The proposition I offer is that *the larger the number of social variables which confront industry and management, the greater the power of the designer.*

Without a doubt the most difficult of these many variables, as we approach what Daniel Bell calls the "post-industrial society," is the matter of values. Bell asserts that:

> The social structure today is ruled by an economic principle of rationality, defined in terms of efficiency in the allocation of resources; the culture, in contrast, is prodigal, promiscuous, dominated by an anti-rational, anti-intellectual temper. The character structure inherited from the nineteenth century—with its emphasis on self-discipline, delayed gratification, restraint—is still relevant to the demands of the social structure; but it clashes sharply with the culture, where such bourgeois values have been completely rejected.[4]

Finally, Bell suggests that:

> ... contrary to Marx's idea of culture "reflecting" an economy, integrally tied to it through the exchange process, two distinct and extraordinary changes are taking place. Art has become increasingly autonomous, making the artist a powerful taste-maker in his own right; the "social location" of the individual (his social class or other position) no longer determines his life-style and his values.[5]

Any reader of Toffler's *Future Shock* is urged to read his introduction to an earlier collection of essays, *Values and the Future*.[6] In it Toffler notes not only that we do not know what our young people will be thinking a decade from now, but also that we do not even know what the establishment itself will be thinking. This means, among many other things, that predictions about tomorrow are less translatable into the charts and tables that always intrigue executives. This leads to our fourth component of design.

By *critique*, our last major component, I refer to an ongoing dialogue between honesty and falsity, between the episodic and the permanent, between the easy-because-familiar solution and the difficult-because-unknown variables. The proposition that derives from this has already been evident among proponents of the futuristic movement—Kahn, de Jouvenal, Junkh, Fuller, etc.—and *moves the analysis into large models, systems, syntheses, integrations, and holistic patterns, as distinct from fragments.*

It is clear, for example, that the basic needs or bases for work are undergoing serious modification. The miracle, and the potential, of mass production and "mass culture," which many intellectuals abjure, is to make accessible to the masses what was once the prerogative of the rich. Indeed, our class structure is the converse of that of traditional Europe: There, the powerful were amateurs at work and experts at play, but our business leaders, for the most part, know only how to work, lacking a knowledge, interest, or skill in literature, the arts, or activities possessing nonwork values. The general culture, which has been designed for efficient production and often ineffective living, is now being re-examined, whether in the San Francisco attack on mindless traffic and higher buildings, or in the growth of adult education throughout the nation. Aspirations for *things* are now being supplemented by aspirations for *lifestyles* in which there may be less anxiety, more access to time, better racial and human relationships, moves to the suburbs, pollutant-free waterways, and more emotional security as people approach older age.

The major components of the leisure model are also fourfold, as we have seen in the model described earlier: *conditions, selection, functions,* and *meanings.*

Let us now apply the hypothesis of fusions which was extracted from the model for the purposes of Chapter 8 moving from the Conquest to the Cultivated social order.

The impact on design work is the *flexibility* which these fusions suggest. The stages of life, a hangover from early industrialization—childhood, school, work, death—have already been enlarged in recent decades by a combination of retirement and longer life. The four-day work week is only one model, and a very simple one, which has broken a habit of industrial structure, and is assisted by computerized inventories and manpower planning; it is also a testament to what management should have known long ago—that people produce better when they have some control over work–leisure rhythms, moods, family organization, or seasons.

Simultaneous patterns may be anticipated—going to school and working during the same year: flexible patterns emerge when the line between work and retirement is minimized or eliminated, so that one travels or takes intermittent sabbaticals while she/he is involved and healthy, or before having a family; one works in her/his 60's and 70's, and pays the interest on the *time* she/he borrowed, by work energy, exactly as one now repays the money she/he borrows. Inflation, even if not as dramatic as we have known, will persist; to state it differently, the dollar is no more a standard of measurement with any constancy over the years. We must relearn our fundamental economics, equating real income with *access*—to time, distance, health services, people, literacy, images of the world, and so on. In my own leisure model, I have left out the word "economics," and deal with the energy system. Speaking of alternatives, for the same reasons that money is worth *less*, the *hour* is worth more in its potential to provide this access.

These flexibilities obviously have their implications—for the economy, educational patterns, family life, community functions, consuming patterns, and personal tastes. Indeed, they may provide a radical transformation beyond any political program. I shall briefly discuss only one example from each leisure component, relating each to the design field.

1. Flexibility in lifestyles assumes a new *condition* of chronological age, with a recognition that *every age has its physical limitations and its socio-psychological potentials, increasingly free from the definition of others*. This is already clearly evident with the elderly, who have previously responded to the traditional perception of them by others. Now they are in the process of asserting that "Old Is Beautiful," with political and behavioral consequences. Retirement complexes stuck away in isolated rural or fringe areas are relics of "medieval" life. One may foresee the mingling of generations in, for example, schools where programs, rooms, and teaching devices are applicable to three generations simultaneously. This is one rationale for the flexible use of space—in homes, institutions, schools, and community planning. Examples of such useful thinking in the design of human resource centers are found in a report by Pfeiffer Associates of New York, with the help of the Ford Foundation.[7] An example of archaic thinking is the federally funded housing complex built in St. Louis which jammed thousands of poor together with almost no recreational spaces; it was eventually torn down. So the age differentiation will decline in the decades ahead.

2. The *selection* of leisure activities will be influenced increasingly by *indoor–outdoor fusions in lifestyles, and, therefore, demand an integration of urban and regional planning which is presently lacking*. In view of the fact that as a nation we have only recently come from rural life, it is surprising how little we have been able to integrate the characteristic elements of urban life and nature. Paolo Soleri's "arcology" is an attempt to find this fusion in a compact community, Arcosanti, in the Arizona desert.

An example of the new leisure *dynamics* is *the increase and changing nature of travel, which suggests a new design philosophy*. Domestic and international travel are dramatic aspects of new leisure patterns, less limited by expense, time, and social class patterns. Its two phases are the travel itself and the nature of the destination; the emerging business aspect is the "packaging" or interrelationship of the two. The second of these—illustrated by the nature, preparation, and preservation of tourist destinations—is now the subject of considerable study. For example, Varna, Bulgaria, on the Black Sea has a so-called Golden Sands area about 10 miles north of the city where the modernistic hotels were constructed on the hills with a rational relationship of beach, roads, gardens, restaurants, and walking areas that serve the public and protect privacy in a way completely foreign to Miami Beach or Atlantic City. Similarly, extensive care is being taken along the Dalmation coast of Yugoslavia to carry out a functional and aesthetic pattern of development for the inevitable tourism ahead. There, as here, a conflict has clearly developed between bringing people and yet preserving that which they come to see. In Sarasota, Florida, for example, a community committed to gracious living for the affluent, about 50 miles of public shoreline have been reduced to 35 over the last decade, with condominium developers presently attempting to build on seven more miles of shoreline.

The juxtaposition of these models—one for design, one for leisure—leads us into a final set of considerations. My first inclination is to subdivide these into the public and the private sectors. On further thought, here, too, I find a dramatic fusion of interests and even of structure. Less and less is public policy in a position to provide the opportunities for creative leisure: The federal parks are jammed, forcing quotas on attendance; municipalities, forced to cut down on budgets, often start cutting recreational facilities; on all levels the arts are minimized or neglected as budgetary allocations; libraries reduce their services.

Yet the answers are not to be expected from the governmental levels, even if we renamed one cabinet office the Department of Labor and Leisure. Rather, one can look forward to innovative syntheses of public and private. Already we see private corporations moving toward their own positions on *developing* as well as *employing* a whole person. Already, a number of large companies have established "retreats" where, on land that they own, they can design facilities and provide opportunities for quiet, for contemplation, for relief from the massive complexities of work life. For several decades, corporations have invested considerable sums in the liberal arts education of their executives, sending them to schools, to seminars, to the Bethels and the Aspens. The labor unions are also moving in the same broader directions, feeling some responsibility for the use of free time for which they properly take some credit.

There is also movement in the more public-minded orientation of private land. For example, a large power firm in one of our southern states is presently developing a multi-purpose plan for 8,000 acres, incorporating areas for counselling, the arts, education, fishing, camping, and so on. But in addition, the proposal includes a plan for executives whose contract would provide a dual living arrangement, with the family residing in the rural area, and the employee spending as little time as needed in the central city office.

There are many forms that the fusion of good design and creative leisure might take in the lifestyles for 2000 A.D.—in both the private and the public sectors or in syntheses of the two: joint development of land and creation of innovative communities; cross-fertilization of skills in public and private mass media; enlarged corporation support for the arts; credit plans in sabbaticals from work for public service; adult education centers funded by labor, management, and tax structure.

What is at stake in all of this is indicated in the warning given by Thoreau to an America of an earlier age that we might become the tool of our own tools. The answers are no longer found in isolation by one discipline or another, by one benefactor or by one foundation or another. The design field cuts across an enormous range of skills, interests, and public and private advocacy. Leisure, in the large sense, brings to it not merely a new market which already represents about one-fifth of our economy, but also a heaven for those whose cosmological commitments extend no further than the next plane to Miami. Some such fusion of models that has been proposed between the two is long overdue.

CHAPTER 11

Business, Labor, and the Four-Day Work Week

"Attention workers! The four-day week is here at last!" is the way Richard W. McManus began a story September 4, 1971, in the *Christian Science Monitor*. Five months later, for the same distinguished paper, he began his economic review, "A three-day week—a 12-hour day." Between these accounts a *Monitor* editorial observes, "Perhaps nothing registers the rate of technological progress—what it takes to provide the basic wants and needs of life—better than the shrinkage of the workweek."

The recent Chrysler–UAW contract calls for getting ready to install a pilot four-day week. Riva Poor's book, *4 Days, 40 Hours: Reporting a Revolution in Work and Leisure*, notes that about 11,000 employees—usually in small companies—are trying out some formula of squeezing the typical 40-hour work week into a new time structure: Samsonite luggage makers work 38 hours, Monday through Thursday; in Everett, Massachusetts, employees of Kyanize Paints start at 7:00 A.M. and leave at 4:30 P.M. with no coffee breaks; a firm in Cushing, Oklahoma, stays open seven days a week, but each employee works only four; a retail tire company in Los Angeles is open Thursdays through Saturdays, when sales are best.[1]

Almost everywhere the reports are favorable from workers and employers alike. As a *Wall Street Journal* report summarized the evaluations in a dispatch of October 15, 1970:

> The workers love it, which is less than surprising. . . . What is surprising, though, is that the employers love it, too. The four-day week . . . increases productivity, decreases absenteeism, boosts worker morale and cuts worker turnover.

105

The 40-hour week itself is undergoing serious reconsideration. Mutual and Metropolitan insurance companies are both trying the three-day week for their data-processing staffs (40 and 460 men, respectively) to maximize use of expensive computers. Sylvia Porter puts the challenge of new time to the worker in her column of February 16, 1975: "How will you handle yourself when '5-40' gives way to '4-40' and then swings into '4-32'?"

When the Leisure Studies Program at the University of South Florida was established in 1967 to deal precisely with these issues, we were no oracles. The "handwriting on the wall" has been in neon signs for anyone to read: the rise in affluence for the great bulk of population; the rising GNP; aspirations of the masses for goods and services related to leisure (comprising about 15 percent of our total consuming expenditures); the desire for longer vacations; the complete retirement of 60 percent of our 20 million citizens over 65; the increasing lure of the outdoors for riding, picnicking, and fishing; continual creation of computers as the world's fastest-moving industry; movements into the more comfortable milieu of the suburbs; and so on and so on.

Sylvia Porter's question, addressed to each of us as employees, is too narrow. The question of how we will respond to, use, and demand the "4-32" formula must in large part be answered by the whole society.

As to program areas such as adult education, the arts, libraries, and the mass media, the trend, especially among youth (whose values may still prevail in the decades ahead), is toward personal growth, fulfillment, and significance, and toward a society that is rich in meaning as well as in things. The thoughts of youth today may provide major clues as to whether adult workers of tomorrow will trade income for time.

As to government at all levels, the use of the new time as a new option for the many will depend in part on the alternatives that are provided, such as museums, parks, camp sites, imaginative playgrounds, sports arenas, educational facilities, community centers, and symphonies.

As to labor, unions are already negotiating on an annual basis. The work year was roughly 3,000 hours in 1900—and 2,000 now. The four-day week is far more than it appears to be on the surface; in a decade or two, negotiations may well turn on a life-plan contract: if, for example, one is to work 1,500 hours annually for 20 years, or a total of 30,000 hours, the employee might want to distribute these hours flexibly, taking long sabbaticals when she/he is young and working more in her/his 60's and 70's. (Biologists are predicting a "normal" life to 95 in the near future.)

It seems that employers, the American business leaders and industrialists, are ignoring the elementary truism that the employee is most effective when she/he has maximum control over the distribution of her/his work and nonwork time; there is something nonsensical (with modern communications as a basis for new interfacing in functional roles) about having millions all at work between 9 and 5—wasting hours of sunshine, clogging the roads, and squeezing everyone into a rigid time structure.

Yet industrial management is slow to learn and, judging from recent negotiations, it will probably continue to take a traditional stand for some time. In late 1977, legislation was pending in the Congress to remove a mandatory retirement age for federal employees and to raise the retirement age to 70 in private industry; several states have already passed similar lifetime employment for their state employees. The California Senate, on November 1, 1977, held its first hearings on a "leisuring-sharing bill," to enlarge leisure periods in both governmental and private work as a device for providing more jobs for the employed. These discussions may have the impact of forcing a reconsideration of work patterns in general.

"The question of more leisure time is certainly going to be an issue," a spokesperson for the then 1.6-million-member United Auto Workers Union said on November 26, 1972. "Practically all of the nation's officers have indicated in one way or another that more time off to allow the worker to be with his family is essential. "This reduction of work time could take various forms, ranging from more paid holidays to sabbaticals tied to an accumulation of reduced work hours, the spokesperson continued. One proposal that union leaders have tossed out as "food for thought" involves setting aside 10 percent of the work year for each production employee. Crediting an employee with four hours of leisure time a week—10 percent of a 40-hour week—would give her/him 26 days at the end of the work year, or one week per quarter.

The auto industry, running full throttle with a record demand for new cars, has become increasingly reluctant to shut down its multi-billion dollar production apparatus for holidays. Idle capacity is costly for an industry in which the four biggest producers—General Motors Corporation, Ford Motor Company, Chrysler Corporation, and American Motors—turned out over 19,660,000 passenger cars in 1975, or an average of 37,000 cars daily. That was the reason Ford executives cited in refusing to give its 160,000 hourly workers a Thanksgiving weekend in 1972. And in an annual report to its stockholders, they also stated that:

> Any impairment of management's ability to schedule the full use of facilities—whether it is the result of absent workers, more holidays, work stoppages, four-day weeks, arbitrary limits on overtime, or some other cause—is enormously expensive.

UAW Vice-President Ken Bannon, in charge of the union's Ford department, had asked Ford's management to shift a bonus holiday slated for December 17, a Sunday, to the Friday after Thanksgiving, thus putting together a long weekend for most workers. The company refused, saying it needed production time.

Eight of the auto industry's ten holidays come after September 1, during the peak demand period for new cars and trucks.

Union officials began to sound out local union leaders on their leisure time ideas in 1973. And American industrial management is best advised to listen carefully to the increasing demands for leisure time during forthcoming auto negotiations.

"Instead of opposing labor union demands for more leisure time in the auto negotiations of 1973, management, labor and government should join forces in serious considerations of these new aspirations for time," our Leisure Studies Program noted in a national press release. We reminded business leaders that when Henry Ford introduced the five-day week in 1926, Judge Gary of U.S. Steel called this nonsense; yet four decades later U.S. Steel is the company with the most advanced sabbatical plan—13 weeks paid vacation every five years. "What smaller management is learning from the growing interest in the four-day week," said our public release, "is that production generally goes up when the worker has some control over the planning of his work and his non-work time."

The subject has to be divided into these two parts: the redistribution of work time and the reduction of work hours. Such terms as "work ethic" and "idle capacity" are smokescreens being used by the government and industry to escape the real issues. As to the use of one's time, we noted that while in office President Nixon showed good judgment for his mental health by changing his work setting as often as he did, from Washington to California to Florida. The American worker, who doesn't have this freedom, is moving rapidly toward similar aspirations of winter holidays and longer weekends. From the point of view of the American economy, almost one-fifth of our consumers' dollars are spent for recreational goods and services; naturally the masses want the time to use their color televisions and new cars. Economically and psychologically, a leisure cycle is now in force, where the demands for time and for leisure services feed each other.

Since those statements to the press, the energy crisis came to a dramatic point in early 1974. One effect has been to intensify interest in the shorter work week to save energy. Enforced leisure through unemployment (about 1,000,000 were directly affected by mid-January of 1974) is another economic consequence. However, this was minimal compared to the three-day work week that had already hit England by this time. The structure of work and nonwork time has in the past been dependent on such matters as one's social class, illness, and vacation patterns, and, of course, on general levels of employment. In isolated segments of the work force, the flow of parts or materials also determines work. Carpenters may be useless during those days when essential lumber has not arrived at the building site.

The concern for energy conservation may bring about permanent changes in the business and manufacturing world beyond the transition from large to compact cars. A primary one, I suggest, will result from the interaction of management and labor on new time patterns. Some labor unions have perhaps hindered management's acceptance of the four-day week by maintaining that a 10-hour day (no matter if the week's total is 40) is still 10 hours, and therefore requires two hours of overtime pay. But that attitude will change under pressure from union members themselves.

The fact is that two major factors are now complicating management–labor negotiations: cybernation and leisure. These factors are new to both parties, and since they are closely interrelated, neither can be negotiated or analyzed in isolation from the other. Intermittent leisure and earlier retirement are social ways of approaching technology, and both are powerful motivations for working less. The resolution of the problem will therefore involve mutual agreement between employer and employee, as they jointly come to grips with restructuring of lifestyles—with which neither party has had experience or ideological preparation.

Similarly, in confronting such issues as new flexitime formulas, I anticipate strange partnerships among unions, management, and government. This will come to the fore on such unfamiliar matters as guaranteed annual incomes, lifetime contracts, flexitime floating pension plans, "hour banks," and pre-retirement planning. All this does not mean that labor and management will see eye to eye, for their central interests as negotiators will remain distinct, as they have historically. What will result is a new type of negotiation, with all sides stepping gingerly into new territory. By the end of the century we will have seen much "plowing," and in retrospect the present energy crisis will be viewed as the sowing of additional seeds. New winds in the whole atmosphere, extending beyond even labor and management, will push both of these parties in directions neither had planned or foreseen.

CHAPTER 12

Leisure and the General Process of Theory/Policy

The growth of social science should not imply a singular solution to problems of "theory" and "policy," to thought–application, talk–action, or similar references and pairings. Debate and consciousness of some continuum from the realm of discourse to that of decision, action, or implementation are implicit with all social organization since the beginning of humanity, and they have always taken place in families, tribes, work groups, and the infinite variety of social structures. Ancient civilizations and rulers dealt with these dichotomies when they called upon sages for advice or carried on debates among themselves before undertaking wars. An objectification of political processes reached a high level with Aristotle and—within his own framework of moral goals—Machiavelli.

Certainly, one of the consequences of the enormous sums invested by governments and foundations in "pure" research since World War II was a mood of reckoning about the results of such expenditures. In the United States, for example, President Lyndon Johnson's request for a social accounting led to special conferences among "hard-core" physical scientists, reheating the familiar issues regarding their roles and responsibilities. The social sciences are less capable of demonstrating their usefulness, with such notable exceptions as the theorists investigating public opinion and the market research pollsters working for politicians and businesses.

If, as has been said, a remarkable characteristic of our time in history is "the invention of invention," then perhaps the combination of the social sciences with policy formulation has created the *evaluation of evaluation*. What social scientists attempt to do is to test the goals and assumptions that are integral to policy by a conceptualization of the whole process that moves from "problem" to "policy." In the most general terms—and hardly ever in the simple succession to be noted here—the continuum that penetrates all policy (in a tribal meeting or in a parliament) embraces these phases:

1. A feeling arises that something needs attention; that a "problem" exists; as for "crime," for instance, sociologists or the FBI produces *data*. The data confirm that something needs to be done.

2. The data, gossip, or perception is interpreted *vis-a-vis* some *perspective, ideology, norm, standard,* or *philosophy;* facts never "speak for themselves," but always fit into some prior or imposed construct of the nonproblematic condition.

3. Based on the recognition of the "problem"—i.e., the gap between what is and what should be—a *decision* is made by the king, sheriff, university regents, Congress, or Mother; the "policy" can, therefore, range from a decision to spank to the establishment of a new tax.

4. *Implementation* may follow or it may *not* as when the U.S. Congress does not appropriate essential funds to realize the decision it has reached. However, usually the spanking does crystallize after Mother's decision, or the jail term does follow a judge's sentencing.

5. *Evaluation*—sometimes—is formally made; informal evaluation is practically *always* made following any decision to act either on a personal level or on a national scale: (1) "I'm glad I took the new job"; (2) "The new law to save our town from pollution is succeeding."

The student of social or personal policy is interested in more than a spelling out of such items in the continuum. At least three issues confront her/him. First, she/he is concerned with the dynamics within each of these five components; for example, what are the origins of the philosophy? Second, how are the bridges established between the various elements of the process: the relevant roles, rules, traditions, bureaucratic barriers, communications, or levels of information? Third, what are the interrelationships of the various policies to the whole, i.e., of policies about crime, education, tax structure, energy controls, etc., to the national values of the United States in the mid-1970's?

Studies of leisure now proceeding in many parts of the world illustrate the points above. Since World War II, there has been a pronounced interest in this subject in all industrial nations—indeed, among so-called underdeveloped nations as well. They have all seen the impact of technology on changes in work structures, the aspiration for more time free from work, the increase in the number of cars, the enormous growth in uses of the mass media, the trends toward earlier retirement, and the larger expenditures for recreation. The past 15 years have, therefore, witnessed a growth in research in universities, government offices, and such private quarters as marketing agencies and manufacturers of recreational equipment; also many conferences—regional, national, and international—have been held.

The *data* are clear: productivity increases under industrialization, earlier retirement, and longer vacations. *Philosophy* in the use of these data is highly unclear, perhaps involving the substitution of what Havighurst and others call the "leisure ethic" for the work attitudes that hang on from the past. *Policy* is similarly unclear as to how labor unions should negotiate *vis-a-vis* flexitime and the spread of work hours; educational policy has almost ignored the relevant data, and thus does not know how to develop appropriate attitudes. *Implementation* is cloudy, as the leaders of adult education, gerontology, and recreation still seek new programs for their clients and better curricula for their students. *Evaluation* is the most unclear of all as we seek to weigh "happiness" in general, "adjustment" for the retiree, or "equity" for those disemployed by cybernation.

As to the clarification of bridges from one of these to the other, Dr. Claudine Attias-Donfut of Paris and I went through an example of the difficulty. As co-editors of a special issue of *Society and Leisure* on the subject of leisure and the elderly (the "third age," to use the favorite European term), we decided to invite papers on current or recent research on the issue of "bridges." The directive to our authors is reproduced in the published issue; addressing ourselves to gerontologists, we noted that:

> The profession has its own theoreticians, but it is primarily a complex of persons and agencies who are responsible for governmental programs, nursing homes, and a variety of other "real" situations. Those who create policy or administer programs are not unaware of theoretical studies on aging or on leisure; like policy or program makers in all fields, they rely heavily on experience, common sense, or intuition; aided (often spasmodically) by the professional journals, which they may (or may not) read, and the conferences which they may (or may not) attend. Their need for the help of scientists of leisure is real, with the rapidity of changes they confront.[1]

As an aid to the formulation of principles, we reproduced the generalizations of the American sociologist James Coleman.[2] Further to assist the authors, we postulated a total of 11 specific questions under the supposition either (a) that the scientific study was commissioned or suggested by a policy or administrative agency, or (b) that the scientific study was concerned and executed largely or entirely by the group of leisure scholars.

Although the resulting papers from various countries were valuable for their content, little if anything was addressed to the subject—*bridges* from theory to policy! Of course, much the same might have happened had we dealt with any other subject; yet the leisure field—especially as it relates to the elderly—offers a relatively direct opportunity for applications because of the number of applied areas that are affected by changes to an increasingly nonwork or lesser-work lifestyle.

Finally, leisure studies inherently integrate a range of issues that cut across and move into the micro-, macro-, and mid-range issues, as I have sought to demonstrate in my model. While these statements have not exhausted the theoretical issues of theory/policy, they do set the stage for later generalizations based on the current Polish experience.

In November 1974, I had the privilege of meeting for 10 days in Poland with various teams of researchers and individual scholars whose major areas of interest lie in studies of leisure.[3] Aside from formal meetings with groups or teams, I spent many hours in informal conversations or social gatherings (which in Polish history—whether in homes or cafes—have long played an important role in molding opinion among intellectuals).

Poland's recent world importance and economic expansion are first noted: In 1970 it produced almost 40 percent of Europe's sulphur, almost 15 percent of its hard coal, and almost 5 percent of its sea-going ships. In 1974 exports increased 20 percent over those in 1973, with a 40 percent growth in exports to nonsocialist nations. The 1973–1974 industrial development equalled that of the total previous five-year period. Suffering from the energy crisis less than many other countries, Poland's sales of domestic products in the first quarter of 1974 exceeded by almost 12 percent those of the same period of the year before. Building, for instance, went up in comparable periods by over 20 percent. The total income of the Polish population during the year rose about 17 percent.[4]

Following the well-known revolt among shipbuilders, this expansion in consumer goods was in part a reaction to new political policies. For our purpose, it is to be noted that a planned economy must place a high value on accurate data about its own resources, needs, and social trends—a point often ignored by western public opinion. Questions arise: What resources are put into the data-gathering process (as in the purchase of computers or the training of programmers)? What policy decisions are made for the use of such data (within the political "conflicts and compromises" to which Rokkan refers)?[5]

Thus, a special interest may be found in a statement by Edward Gierek, the First Secretary of the Polish United Workers Party's Central Committee. Noting that 1973 was the year of Polish science, Gierek said, "We must work out and introduce in practice an effective programme of a harmonious combination of scientific research efforts with a long-range development programme of the economy." On the same occasion, Jan Szydlak, PUWP Secretary, noted in more specific terms:

> Viewed against this background, the standing of the system of social sciences grows in importance as a base for theoretical research, helping to shape party strategy, which gives concrete shape to

upbringing programmes and adds substance to our party argumentation. The programme outlined by the VI Congress and the overall shape of the policy practiced by our party established a propitious climate for general development of the social sciences. As a result, we noted significant progress in drawing social sciences increasingly into the practical service of society.[6]

The opportunity presented itself to explore high-level intentions more directly in Warsaw during two hours that I spent with Minister of Work, Wages, and Social Affairs Bralczyski. He was flanked by two staff members (one responsible for new investments for outdoor recreation, the other concerned with wage and hour policies); also present was Dr. Edmund Wnuk'-Lipinski, who headed a research team responsible to the Minister.[7]

This ministry was only established in 1972. Although political policies relating to work and nonwork time had been established previously, the recent recognition of "new weapons"—i.e., new policies as well as data and research—resulted in the establishment of a "social fund" to help give direction to leisure enterprises, such as social centers. An example of another "tool" is the establishment of central libraries throughout the country designed to provide newspapers, journals, and books on an international level. Electronic data resources are being established, with the cooperation of ILO, to keep abreast of world scientific materials and research.

The Minister listed three obstacles in these efforts.

a. Social consciousness: society is not accustomed to extended leisure periods or its uses;

b. Governmental structure: older established agencies that are related to such issues are hard to change, such as the Ministries of Culture and of Trade (his office was therefore established as a coordinating agency);

c. Funds: other needs (pensions, housing, etc.) are also pressing for attention, incomes are low, and fee structures for recreational services must be limited, while simultaneously the level of life goes up.

All of these difficulties will decline in the future, but the Minister says that "convincing proposals" are needed both to arrive at political decisions and to achieve public support and "pressures."

The opportunity could not be ignored to raise questions about political processes with the Minister, bearing in mind a relevant comment made by Mr. Gierek in the speech quoted above:

> In accordance with our practice to date, we shall so organize state work and political life as to make every party member and every citizen, every worker, farmer and intellectual able to take part in the shaping of

developmental concepts of Poland. Only in this manner will the collective wisdom of the nation be embodied in our development programme.

My question, therefore, was: Is there a realistic opportunity for policy pressures to develop from within the society, eventually affecting decisions at the top?

As to the use of the democratic process, the Minister's reply emphasized that ideas and pressures already come from below; further, "by creating facilities we create needs, but this takes time." The research, by Dr. Wnuk'-Lipinski and others, is intent on finding what the population wants and what it needs, as well as how it acts. Organized groups constitute an important influence. "Social consciousness is determined by the social reality." Poland, he noted, does more social research than the other socialist societies.

An interesting thought was suggested by these replies, reinforced as they were by the heavy demand for social research (verified in close conversations with the researchers themselves)—that perhaps the research community, through this invitation to sound out the nation, is actually engaged in a cautious preliminary step toward a conscious democratic influence. If, indeed, the sociological studies show that the public wants more consumer goods, this would not in itself imply a criticism of the socialist system. What about *time,* a new demand also in the West, as evident in the labor negotiations of the past few decades? If Polish workers seemed overly anxious for more hours away from work, a serious issue might arise for socialist philosophy. One of the questions I put to the Minister was whether there is not a "natural antagonism" between the traditional socialist ideological emphasis on work and the very recent interest in leisure? His reply was that there is no theory of leisure under socialism, that "connections" now have to be made. The image of the socialist citizen, he observed, is "active." Leisure can be seen in this light as an enrichment of the whole person, the "new person." Again, he returned to the tool of social research, because under socialism "recommendations based on data can be implemented." Indeed, based on just such studies, Polish workers have had, since 1975, their number of "free Saturdays" increased from 6 to 12 per year! What the population is doing with this new increment of time has become the immediate object of considerable research.

I must confess that this research "problem" of the new Saturdays for leisure struck me at first as somewhat extraneous. Yet, the American, typically used to 52 such Saturdays, is, after all, asking a similar question *vis-a-vis* the additional Friday in the growing four-day work pattern! Nor can the outsider remark that "there is no problem"—no matter how many free days are opened up to nonwork preoccupations—if there are sufficient alternatives for activity or participation, on the assumption that every person will somehow adapt. For now there are other questions: What is the relation of adaptation of free-time use to knowledge of opportunities, to one's "personality," to one's circle of acquaintances, to the nature of one's work habits and values? Those social scientists already admitted into the parlors of policy perhaps do well to maximize the risks of rapid change at the same time that they uncover and articulate the growth of new consumer demands and of emerging lifestyles. A real issue for "active" or "concrete" sociology is that it remains useful for policymakers only as long as it strikes an operational balance between data and debate. Apparently the acknowledged lack of leisure "theory" in Poland has not yet produced a conviction among the social scientists there that more time is, *ipso facto,* desirable.

Here, then, is the dilemma in the theory/policy continuum that seems to emerge from the current Polish experience:

The given situation for social scientists in Poland:

1. The political leadership is actively looking for new social directions.

2. The ministers in charge of administration and policy formulation are encouraged to draw on researchers.

3. The researchers in the leisure field are invited—indeed, expected—to contribute:

   a. to cultural policy directions,

   b. to knowledge of what the population does in its leisure and what it wants to do,

   c. to analysis of new work experiments such as flexitime.

The dilemma for social scientists in Poland:

1. The sudden demand (only since 1970) to come up with both general theory and specialized data.

2. The problem of developing a leisure theory:

   a. which is in accord with socialist theory,

   b. which is related to the mainstream of western social science,

   c. which is both action-oriented and "pure,"

   d. which is microcosmic, middle-range, and macrocosmic, and all at once,

   e. which is multi-disciplinary.

3. The problem of so studying the Polish population that the results reveal what the present leisure practices or "needs" are and how potential patterns will develop without prior models for the public to observe.

In facing this series of situations and dilemmas, the institutionalization of Polish social science provides some clues to possible outcomes. Broadly seen, the Polish Academy of Science contains teams in the various disciplines that are relatively free to select research problems; and each of the ministries has related institutes, with scholars whose teams work on more immediate issues for the ministry, obtaining less scholarly prestige but higher salaries. If the theorists in the Academy may be presumed to be conceptualizing in the sense of developing directions as well as in defining research, then Joffre Dumazedier's model for leisure policy is strikingly met. In his latest volume, *Sociology of Leisure,*[8] the eminent French scholar lists the following roles as essential for action in the leisure field: the research worker, the cultural expert, the administrator, and the politician. As to the first, Dumazedier advocates an "active sociology," so that the researcher not only lets the subjects of the inquiry "in on the feedback of his inquiry, he associates them to all its phases. He thus contributes to the progress of rationality in the thought processes of men of action." The author speaks of the "cultural expert" role—the person who "is best qualified to propose the values a cultural policy should promote, with regard to creation, dissemination or the participation of the public." We may assume that in such an institutional arrangement as the Polish scholarship enjoys, members of the Academy may properly assume the "cultural expert" role, largely because they are permitted to define their function. Indeed, Dr. Anna Olszewska, leader of leisure research in the Academy, is presently preparing a book-length position paper in which she deals explicitly with values and national goals; further, she is secretary of a national task force headed by Dr. Jan Sczcepanski which has been given the assignment of defining Poland's "changes in culture, consumption, leisure, and system of values." The outsider may safely assume, therefore, that Academy and institute scholars can be working on similar research problems; the real distinction lies in the "cultural" breath of the former, their explicit concern with goals, and the tendency for relating to other disciplines which a value orientation necessitates. Those Polish scholars who are affiliated with institutes, on the other hand, are deeply involved in more traditional research tasks that tie them closely to empirical studies in other countries.

The roles of *administrator* and *politician* are self-evident in the Polish situation. In western society, these roles are less distinct; we are inclined to think of the politician as the first of these two steps, with the administrator as the implementor. In the Polish structure, the post-1970 caution of political action arises from the greater heed of internal pressures, which may run contrary to national political policy *vis-a-vis* other socialist nations, particularly the USSR.

Another characteristic of Polish sociology is the nature of administrative leadership. Thus, the head of the Institute for Philosophy and

Sociology, Dr. Jan Sczcepanski, is a scholar of world standing. In his other roles as assistant director of the Academy and as an elected member of the Polish parliament, Dr. Sczcepanski's views on the place of social science scholarship in formulating national policy are singularly relevant.

The basic concern of all theorists and researchers is whether their studies and recommendations will be read, studied, and seriously considered by top officials. Americans still have a vivid memory of national commissions appointed by Presidents—on pornography, civil rights, crime, national goals, etc.—and ignored. Sczcepanski, on the other hand, chaired a national commission to revise the educational system; the commission's work was completed in 1973; its findings were considered and debated in 1974; its proposals were implemented in 1975. Leisure scholars are presently participating in a new national task force on consumption patterns and lifestyles. The previous experience bears out the earlier statements by Edward Gierek; the sense of participation by social scientists in the current effort can be imagined. Sczcepanski is acutely conscious of the search for scientific objectivity and the necessity for a conceptualization of the research role *vis-a-vis* implementation. This does not imply a rigid organizational separation; indeed, there are academic scholars on the nation's Planning Commission.

To generalize on the Polish case study, no one has yet developed a classification of "problems" or "issues" that relate to leisure. Perhaps the time has not arrived. Overt issues can be specified, such as the uses of time, expenditures, or planning of public facilities. More covert or underlying issues are definable: new aspirations for discretionary time, relationships of "free time" to the restructuring of work or to such institutions as family and education. In Poland, the concern over the doubling of free Saturdays appears to the outsider as a *short-range* issue; the allocation of national investments is surely a *long-range* matter. To these dichotomies we might add a third, the relation of leisure policy to the *humanistic* and the *technological*. Iran may be used as an illustration of the last.

Even before the recent upheavals by which the oil-producing and exporting countries (OPEC) have become the dominant concentration of world capital, Iran had concluded that its cultural problem was to strike a balance between the model of western life and the preservation of its Islamic art and tradition. The plan to achieve this, announced by the Shah, is noted:

> The discussions and debates which led to the delineation of the principal aspects of Iran's cultural policy became the occasion of a new cultural awareness among the participants. On the one hand, this self-awareness was coupled with a return to the past, and on the other, with a rejection of unpleasant manifestations of Western cultural influence. The growing influence of Western culture in Iran, the reception of this, the search for a suitable antidote to it, and the preservation of the

nation's identity, were questions which formed the core of these discussions. . . . The cultural policy of Iran chose the path of balance in this situation by making its goal the preservation of Iran's culture and its alignment with the conditions of the present.[9]

Leisure in the contemporary world moves ideally in both directions—toward the maintenance and understanding of nature and the handicrafts as well as toward the unabashed use of electronic and transportation facilities.

On another level, especially in nations younger than Iran, and where the many cultural and leisure facilities are developed as part of the profit-making economy, it is often the public segment that stresses the old (as in the preservation of parks) and the private sector that pushes the new (as in the mass media).

Poland's experience highlights the importance of political ideology as one crucial issue for leisure policy. In American terms one might refer to the issue as *commercial* vs. *public:* Presumably, the commercially-oriented leisure (which comprises about 80 percent of recreational activity in the United States) represents the private interest and the public-oriented leisure represents the collective interest. In a thoroughly socialist society, there is little or no "commercial" entity for providing leisure goods or services; there is, of course, private discrimination in the selection and use of available resources. Organized effort is conceivable by action groups to enlarge the private domain, with little or no success at the development of privately owned profit-making services. A capitalist society such as the United States has not reached the relative balance of private/public to be found in the mixed economies of Scandinavia or in the variety of systems of west central Europe, but the direction of leisure facilities seems to be increasingly toward more public ownership and control of facilities. In the United States the Amtrak railroad system is a combined federal and private corporation; our 707 commercial television stations are somewhat balanced by the public stations; our national, state, county, and local park acreage far outweighs the total of commercial parks, resorts, and amusement areas.

The Polish report—referring to the public statements of its post-1970 leadership—suggests a greater reliance on attitudes and wishes of the public as to what the government should provide. This is a far step, of course, from democratic control, for we may assume that the public demand will not be allowed to exceed the basic political limits or structure, although the analysis of Poland above suggests that current research bodies are in an unusual position to discover and report all demands that may deviate from past practices.

These observations suggest that although planners of leisure function within the traditions of their social and political systems, these systems are in the process of significant modification, with the leisure phenomenon as an increasing tool and manifestation of change. Expenditures for commercial recreation may be expected to decline in the next few years as living costs (including gas and oil) go up. Simultaneously, however, interest in nonwork patterns will paradoxically grow—as in the socialist, work-oriented societies—so that national planners in all societies must look to other indices than expenditures for an understanding of the emerging leisure milieu. The work ethic is doomed as machines are applied to carry out the dirty and tiring and repetitive tasks; socialist or capitalist ideology will not stand in the way.

This implies a shift of the problem from *culture* as such to the more inclusive concept of *leisure culture;* what this conceptual enlargement does is to combine *process and content.* If science and art can live side by side—and, indeed, serve each other—then leisure becomes a pivotal or integrative force between culture and technology. One is, in fact, led to the conclusion that this issue will dominate all others with regard to national leisure planning. In such areas as the United States, the current realization resulting from the energy crisis is that we have overlived, overspent, overlit, and overfed; the necessity for living within our means coincides with the appeal led by youth in the late 1960's for Reich's Consciousness III—i.e., for a return to simple things and to humanistic values as a reaction to overcomplexity and impersonalization.

All industrialized countries have already experienced this confrontation to some degree. It is on smaller issues—uses of time, retirement policies, etc.—that various nations will differ, depending on their traditions or degrees of technology, and their work/nonwork structure. My view is that the success of our emerging theory construction about leisure will depend on how clearly we can see connections between these secondary issues and the major area for which Iran has provided a sharper illustration than Poland.

The Polish case makes clear the reliance of leisure planning on theoretical conceptualization and knowledge. On the level of *national* planning, the European nations as a whole are ahead of the United States. In the democratic societies, the nonprofit, professional organizations are more developed and effective in applying pressure on their respective governmental bodies. In the United States, for example, the National Recreation and Park Association (at least until it discontinued its research branch) could be expected to possess an unequalled body of data as a basis for its recommendations to its members and to governmental agencies.

It may seem that the capitalist society possesses a larger array of agencies that help the public to make decisions on the uses of leisure, especially the manufacturers of equipment. For there is no doubt that such equipment not only *responds* to the desires of its consumers, but also serves as "tastemaker." However, in Poland, as in the other socialist societies, there are agencies that do not exist in nonsocialist nations. For example, labor unions assume responsibility for providing vacation services for their employees at low cost.

Research on decision making is needed from scholars in leisure. Attention is called to the current research on decision making within the family—including decisions about leisure behavior—by the 7-nation team under Dumazedier and Bosserman.

Researchers in Poland are presently dealing with traditional sociological issues: how persons are using their time, perceptions of their needs, trends in work structure, and the like.

An inventory or testing of services delivered enters such studies indirectly, as in a comparison of satisfactions derived from houses of culture (community centers), television, movies, the use of cars for vacations, and so on. It would be possible, in the context of any society, to draw up lists of typical activities—travel, adult education, sports, arts, socializing, etc.—and to note the major agencies that make such experiences possible—schools, churches, unions, clubs, public or private travel facilities. A host of issues then arises with respect to comparative costs, controls over client or user, regulations over services, and trends in types of service—to list just a few.

The concern over the doubling of free Saturdays in Poland suggests that the implementation of national work policies has direct impact on leisure prospects. In this case, the conjunction of two 24-hour periods, forming the "weekend" that is familiar in other countries, is far more than 24 plus 24; the "bulk" time opens opportunities far different than a mere doubling of free time. The Congress of the United States has decreed the change of five national holidays so that these become part of a three-day weekend; these 15 days comprise a distinctive illustration of bulk time.

Thus, the implementation of leisure policy involves legislation or impact on time segments as well as agents of information and service. For instance, in Poland there is a special national fund which makes money available to poor families to be used exclusively for vacations. A longer-range form of implementation consists of the education of school children or adults in the use of time, as in visits to museums; in the United States considerable activity of this type goes on, as in centers for the elderly.

There can be few abstract principles to guide leisure policymakers along these lines. Only in the most general way—and pointing to both eastern and western cultures—can we suggest such principles as the provision for a wide range of tastes or the adequate dispensing of information about alternatives. But the view will be heard that these are principles of a different order than must concern the body of research. However, the Polish example has already set apart those abstract researchers of the Academy from those responsible to administrative bodies. The latter translate the research into programs; in a reasonable period, the success or failure of the decisions will cast an evaluative light on the early research findings. If 1975–1976 is a crucial period for Polish researchers in leisure, 1980–1981 may be such a time of early evaluation; among Polish commissions is one committed to forecasting/planning for 2000 A.D. By the latter date, leisure scholars there, if successful in their general analyses, will have firmly entrenched themselves and led the way for all other socialist societies. The tests of their theories will come through pragmatic applications, not through mere acceptance of theory by other theorists.

Implementation is the means through which goals may be realized. The remarks of Dumazedier are appropriate for bridges to other areas of public policy as well as to the field of his own expertise, leisure:

> . . . the relationship between thinking about objectives and thinking about means is renewed . . . has always existed in common sense decision-making, but it has not become more rigorous. To the same objective correspond several possible choices of means. . . . Studies are required to formulate *all possible interventions* in a given field and a given period, and to foresee the likeliest result of each given occurrence. . . . Should priority be given to equipment or to the men who operate it? Should there be more public or more private institutions? And what should the ratio be? . . . Even the problem of nationalization or socialization can now be put in terms of the social or cultural output of the given organization, in connection with development criteria.[10]

The most difficult type of evaluation is that which is the most important—i.e., evaluation of the progress toward the realization of cultural goals. The difficulty arises from (a) the problem of formulating such objectives as "personal growth" in measurable ways that do not obfuscate what are inherently nonmeasurable elements; and (b) the problem of devising the measurement techniques, even with a clearly articulated ("researchable") design. If the decision is made to use criteria other than those that are measurable, a gain is made by involving canons of proof from such fields as philosophy; a loss is expectable from the variety of perspectives and the familiar inability or refusal of different disciplines to talk to each other.

Polish statements of broad objectives are understandably couched in Marxist terms. There is no substantial disagreement from the various socialist sources. An important Czech study states that leisure should be linked with "the transformation of work" and that leisure policy should stimulate subjective wants that are "in harmony with the development of the individual and therefore of the society, too."[11] In Hungary, changes in cultural life call for "more conscious and more purposeful social action" combining empirical study and "social thinking." Such countries—much as they may speak, as did the Minister in Warsaw, of the importance of establishing "new connections" between work and leisure—are perhaps not yet ready to consider leisure itself as a positive cultural entity which carries possibilities of human development separate from work, nurturing human values and providing a basis for genuine creativity. The latter view—leisure as a base for cultural development—is even more difficult to evaluate by any criteria of success. At least the therapeutic view of leisure is somewhat measurable in the success of its antithesis—work.

The ultimate assessment of leisure in any society is a part of larger evaluations of the given culture. Data on use, as in most countries, are now available for such items as time in watching television, the amount of reading, club life, and so on. As isolated bits they are revealing, and more so (as in the Szalai study) when many countries are compared. But ultimately the usefulness of such data must be considered in relation to a nation's own traditions and goals.

A major issue has emerged in all industrialized parts of the world, and in the form of a warning among the less-developed nations: recognition of the stages at which technology becomes counterproductive. Jacques Ellul, Lewis Mumford, and Radovan Richta (and the report of the Czech Academy of Science) have articulated the warning in the broadest levels; environmentalists have been the most conscious of the issue. The concern goes beyond the balance between cultural traditions and technology which was noted in the statement earlier from Iran; in its present form, the question is whether humanism, whether interpersonal relationships, whether "quality" rather than quantity of life can remain inviolate, or whether (as Ellul argues) technology has a momentum of its own that stultifies leisure and all other human expressions. Poland has already reached the point of confrontation, at least in such intellectual centers as Warsaw and Cracow. But the outsider suspects that at this point it remains more on the intellectual level than in places like New York or Tokyo, where pollution of the air and the glut of population have deep impact on attitudes. Leisure serves public policy in such settings as the pivot between the "social structure" and the "cultural life." It is the confrontation of these levels, says Daniel Bell, that will mark the ultimate issue of the post-industrial society.[12]

Notes

Chapter 1

1. Hauser, Philip. "The Chaotic Society: Product of the Social Morphological Revolution." *American Sociological Review* 34; February 1969.
2. Wilensky, Harold. "The Uneven Distribution of Leisure: The Impact of Economic Growth on Free Time." *Work and Leisure.* (Edited by E. O. Smigel.) New Haven, Conn.: College and University Press, 1963.

Chapter 2

1. de Grazia, Sebastian. *Of Time, Work, and Leisure.* New York: The Twentieth Century Fund, 1962.
2. Pieper, Joseph. *Leisure, The Basis of Culture.* New York: Pantheon, 1952.
3. Veblen, Thorstein. *The Theory of the Leisure Class.* New York: Mentor, 1953.
4. Riesman, David. *The Lonely Crowd.* New Haven, Conn.: Yale University Press, 1950.
5. Havighurst, Robert. "Life Styles and Leisure Patterns: Their Evolution Through the Life Cycle." *Leisure and the Third Age.* Paris: International Center of Social Gerontology, Third International Course of Social Gerontology (Dubrovnik), 1972. pp. 35-48.
6. Wilensky, Harold, *op. cit.*
7. Lazarsfeld, Paul. *The People Look at Television.* New York: Knopf, 1963. Lazarsfeld, P.; Berelson, B.; and Gaudet, H. *The People's Choice.* New York: Duell, Sloan & Pearce, 1944.
8. Artemov, V.A.; Bolgov, V.I.; and Vol'skaya, P.V. *Statistica Byudzaetov Uremeni Trudyashchikhsa.* Moscow: Statistica, 1967.
9. Dumazedier, Joffre. *Sociology of Leisure.* Amsterdam: Elsevier, 1974. Introduction.
10. Riesman, David, *op. cit.* Thrasher, F.M. *The Gang.* Chicago: University of Chicago Press, 1936. Becker, Howard—*See* Kaplan, Max. *Leisure in America: A Social Inquiry.* New York: John Wiley, 1960. p. 310. Lynd, R.S., and Lynd, H.M. *Middletown: A Study in American Culture.* New York: Harcourt, Brace, 1929. Lynd, R.S., and Lynd, H.M. *Middletown in Transition.* New York: Harcourt, Brace, 1937. deJager, H. "Listening to the Audience." *Journal of Research in Music Education* XV; Winter 1967.
11. Szalai, A., editor. *The Use of Time.* The Hague: Mouton, 1972.
12. Ozbekan, Hassan. *The Triumph of Technology: "Can" Implies "Ought."* Systems Development Corporation, June 1967. SF-2830.
13. Kreps, Juanita, and Spengler, J.J. "The Leisure Component of Economic Growth." *The Employment Impact of Technological Change.* Vol. II. National Commission on Technology, Automation, and Economic Progress. Washington, D.C.: U.S. Government Printing Office, 1966. Appendix, pp. 353-397. Reproduced in Kaplan, M., and Bosserman, P., editors. *Technology, Human Values, and Leisure.* Nashville: Abingdon, 1971. Appendix A, pp. 239-244.
14. Kahn, Herman, and Wiener, Leonard. *Toward the Year 2000: A Framework for Speculation.* New York: Macmillan, 1967.
15. Gabor, Dennis. *Inventing the Future.* London: Penguin, 1963.

Chapter 3

1. Szalai, A., editor, *op. cit.*
2. Mennell, S.J. *Cultural Policy in Towns.* Strasbourg: Council of Europe, 1975.
3. Kaplan, Max. *Leisure: Theory and Policy.* New York: John Wiley, 1975. Chapter 15.
4. *Documentary Report of the Tanglewood Symposium.* Washington, D.C.: Music Educators National Conference, 1968.
5. Kaplan, Max. *Leisure: Theory and Policy, op. cit.,* Chapter 19.
6. Comfort, Alex. *A Good Age.* New York: Crown Publishers, 1976. p. 24.
7. Rapoport, Robert, and Rapoport, Rhona. *Leisure and the Family Life Cycle.* London: Rutledge and Kegan Paul, 1975.

Chapter 4

1. Priestly, J.B. *Man and Time.* London: Aldus Books, Ltd., 1964.
2. Chekhov, Anton. *The Three Sisters.* New York: Oxford University Press.
3. Bowen, Ada. Unpublished study. Tampa: Leisure Studies Program, University of South Florida, 1970.
4. Szalai, A., editor, *op. cit.*
5. Hartig, Mattias, and Kurz, Ursula. "Some Aspects of Integrative Sociolinguistics." Varna, Bulgaria: International Sociological Association, 1971.
6. Huaco, George A. "The Sociological Model." *The Sociology of Art and Literature: A Reader.* (Edited by M.C. Albrecht, J.H. Barnett, and M. Griff.) New York: Praeger, 1970. p. 549.
7. de Grazia, Sebastian, *op. cit.*
8. Kaplan, Max. *Foundations and Frontiers of Music Education.* New York: Holt, Rinehart & Winston, 1966. pp. 19–20.
9. Kaplan, Max. *Leisure: Theory and Policy, op. cit.,* Chapter 18.
10. Sorokin, P. *Social and Cultural Dynamics.* 4 vols. New York: Harper & Brothers, 1937–1941.
11. Skinner, B.F. *Beyond Freedom and Dignity.* New York: Knopf, 1971. p. 184.
12. Chomsky, Noam. "The Case Against B.F. Skinner." *New York Review of Books,* December 30, 1971. pp. 18–24.
13. Berdyaev, Nicolas. *The Meaning of the Creative Act.* New York: Collier Books, 1962.
14. Bosserman, Phillip. *Technology, Human Values, and Leisure.* (Edited by M. Kaplan and P. Bosserman.) Nashville: Abingdon, 1971. p. 139.
15. Theobald, Robert. "Thinking About the Future." *Technology, Human Values, and Leisure.* (Edited by M. Kaplan and P. Bosserman.) Nashville: Abingdon, 1971. p. 27.
16. Fuller, Buckminster. *Utopia or Oblivion.* New York: Bantam Books, 1969. p. 18.

Chapter 5

1. Szalai, A., editor, *op. cit.*
2. Institute for the Future. *Some Prospects for Social Change by 1985 and Their Impact on Time/Money Budgets.* Middletown, Conn.: the Institute, 1972.
3. Kaplan, Max. *Leisure: Theory and Policy, op. cit.,* Chapter 2.
4. Pieper, Joseph, *op. cit.*
5. Ozbekan, Hassan, *op. cit.*
6. Friedrichs, Robert. *The Sociology of Sociology.* New York: Free Press, 1970.
7. Drucker, Peter. *New York Times,* April 8, 1973.

8. Beier, K., and Rescher, N., editors. *Values and the Future: The Impact of Technological Change on American Values.* New York: Collier–Macmillan, 1970.

9. McLuhan, Marshall. *Understanding Media.* New York: McGraw-Hill, 1965.

10. Kaplan, Max. *Leisure in America: A Social Inquiry.* New York: John Wiley, 1960. Chapter 17.

11. Gottmann, Jean. *Megalopolis: The Urbanized Northeastern Seaboard of the United States.* New York: The Twentieth Century Fund, 1961.

12. Freud, Sigmund. *Beyond the Pleasure Principle.* New York: Boni and Liveright, 1924.

13. Dumazedier, Joffre, *op. cit.*

14. Kaplan, Max. *Leisure, Lifestyle, and Lifespan: Directions for Gerontology.* Philadelphia: W.B. Saunders, forthcoming.

Chapter 6

1. Ellul, Jacques. *The Technological Society.* New York: Vintage Books, 1964.

2. Riesman, David. *Abundance—for What?* New York: Doubleday, 1964.

3. Kahn, Herman, and Wiener, Leonard, *op. cit.*

4. Institute for the Future, *op. cit.*

5. Toffler, Alvin. *Future Shock.* New York: Random House, 1970.

6. Tocqueville, Alexis de. *Democracy in America.* New York: Vintage Books, 1954. Chapter XI.

7. Huizinga, Johann. *Homo Ludens: A Study of the Play Element in Culture.* Boston: Beacon, 1950.

8. Brooklyn Museum. *A Seminar on the Role of the Arts in Meeting the Social and Educational Needs of the Disadvantaged.* HEW Grant #OEG-1-7-070254-2319. Washington, D.C.: U.S. Department of Health, Education, and Welfare, 1967.

9. Brightbill, Charles. *Man and Leisure, A Philosophy of Recreation.* Englewood Cliffs, N.J.: Prentice-Hall, 1961.

10. Kaplan, Max. "We Can Learn Much From the Inner City." *Music Educators Journal* 56: 39–42; January 1970.

11. Sunderland, Jacqueline Tippett. *Older Americans and the Arts.* Washington, D.C.: National Council on Aging, 1973.

Chapter 7

1. Wilensky, Harold, *op. cit.*

2. O'Toole, James, editor. *Work in America.* Cambridge, Mass.: MIT Press, 1974.

3. Best, Fred, and Stern, Barry. *Lifetime Distribution of Education, Work and Leisure: Research, Speculations and Policy Implications of Changing Life Patterns.* Washington, D.C.: George Washington University, Institute for Educational Leadership, 1976.

4. Rapoport, Robert, and Rapoport, Rhona, *op. cit.*

5. Moberg, David. *The Church as a Social Institution.* Englewood Cliffs, N.J.: Prentice-Hall, Inc., 1962. p. 166.

6. Cox, Harvey. *The Feast of Fools.* Cambridge, Mass.: Harvard University Press, 1969. Dahl, Gordon. *Work, Play, and Worship in a Leisure-Oriented Society.* Minneapolis: Augsburg Publishing House, 1972.

7. Pieper, Joseph, *op. cit.*

8. "How Americans Pursue Happiness." *U.S. News and World Report* 60–76; May 23, 1977.

9. Bell, Daniel. *The Coming of Post-Industrial Society.* New York: Basic Books, 1973.

10. Tu Wei-Ming. "The Confucian Perception of Adulthood." *Daedalus* 105; Spring 1976.

Chapter 8

1. Council of Europe. *Past in Future.* Strasbourg: the Council, 1969. p. 6.

2. de Grazia, Sebastian, *op. cit.*

3. Wilensky, Harold, *op. cit.*

4. Veblen, Thorstein, *op. cit.*

5. Ellul, Jacques, *op. cit.*

6. Bell, Daniel, *op. cit.* Toraine, Alain, et al. *Workers' Attitudes to Technical Change.* Paris: OECD, 1965.

7. Richta, Radovan, editor. *Civilization at the Crossroads.* Prague: Czech Academy of Science, 1969.

8. Scheuch, Erwin, and Meyersohn, Rolf. *Soziologie der Freizeit.* Cologne: Krepenheuer & Witsch, 1972.

9. Silbermann, Alphonse. *Vorteile und Nachteile des Kommerziezzen Fernsehens.* Dusseldorf: Econ-Verlag, 1968. Zahn, Ernest. *Die Koszentration de Massenmedien und Ihre Wirkungen.* Dusseldorf: Econ-Verlag, 1970.

10. Kaplan, Max. *Leisure: Theory and Policy, op. cit.,* Chapter 17.

11. Gottmann, Jean, *op. cit.*

12. Lynd, R.S., and Lynd, H.M., *op. cit.*

13. Lundberg, G.A.; Komarovsky, M.; and McIllnery, N.A. *Leisure—A Suburban Study.* New York: Columbia University Press, 1934.

14. Mumford, Lewis. *The City in History: Its Origins, Its Transformations, and Its Prospects.* New York: Harcourt, Brace, 1961. p. 576.

15. McHale, John. *The Future of the Future.* New York: Braziller, 1969.

Chapter 9

1. Private study done by Max Kaplan, et al., for the Walter-Gould Corporation of Sun City Center, Florida, 1974. We found, for example, that among 3,500 residents, as many as 700 were taking weekly Spanish lessons.

2. Leanse, Joyce, project director. *Senior Centers: Senior Group Programs in America.* Washington, D.C.: The National Institute of Senior Centers, 1975.

3. Butler, Robert. *Why Survive? Being Old in America.* New York: Harper & Row, 1975.

4. Znaniecki, Florian. *Cultural Sciences: Their Origin and Development.* Urbana, Ill.: University of Illinois Press, 1952.

5. Benedict, Ruth. *Patterns of Culture.* New York: Houghton Mifflin, 1934.

6. Thomas, W.I., and Znaniecki, F. *The Polish Peasant in Europe and America.* New York: Knopf, 1927. Methodological note.

7. Riesman, David. *The Lonely Crowd, op. cit.*

8. Burke, Kenneth. *A Grammar of Motives.* New York: Prentice-Hall, 1945. Duncan, Hugh. *Language and Literature in Society.* Chicago: University of Chicago Press, 1953.

9. Maslow, A.H. *Motivation and Personality.* 2nd edition. New York: Harper & Row, 1970.

10. de Beauvoir, Simone. *The Coming of Age.* New York: Putnam's Sons, 1972.

11. Johnston, Denis F. "The Future of Work: Three Possible Alternatives." *Monthly Labor Review.* Washington, D.C.: U.S. Department of Labor, May 1972.

12. Woodcock, George. *The Tyranny of the Clock: An Introduction to Social Science.* (Edited by Calhoun, et al.) New York: J.B. Lippincott, 1953. pp. 209–212.

13. Kant, Emanuel. "Transcendental Aesthetic." *Fundamentals of Philosophy*. (Edited by E. Harris.) New York: Rinehart & Winston, 1969. Section II, Chapter 29.

14. Moore, Wilbert. *Man, Time, and Society*. New York: John Wiley, 1963. p. 122.

15. Kreps, Juanita, and Spengler, J.J., *op. cit.*

16. Bosserman, Phillip. *Technology, Human Values and Leisure, op. cit.*, pp. 162–163.

17. Smith, C. Ray. *The American Endless Weekend*. Report by the International Union of Architects, Section of the USA. XI World Congress, Varna, Bulgaria, 1972. p. 106.

18. Richta, Radovan, editor, *op. cit.*

Chapter 10

1. Rodgers, Frank, president of the International Newspaper Syndicate. London, in conversation with the author, 1970.

2. Galbraith, John Kenneth. *The New Industrial State*. Boston: Houghton Mifflin, 1967.

3. Koestler, Arthur. *The Act of Creation*. New York: Dell Publishing Co., 1964. Koestler, Arthur. *The Sleepwalkers*. London: Hutchinson, 1959.

4. Bell, Daniel. *The Public Interest* 18–22; Fall 1970.

5. *Ibid.*

6. Toffler, Alvin. "Introduction." *Values and the Future.* (Edited by K. Beier and N. Rescher.) New York: Collier-Macmillan, 1970.

7. Pfeiffer Associates. *Report to the Brooklyn Institute of Arts and Sciences for a Community Resources Center in East New York*. New York: Pfeiffer Associates, 1971.

Chapter 11

1. Poor, Riva. *4 Days, 40 Hours*. New York: New American Library, 1973.

Chapter 12

1. Kaplan, Max, and Attias-Donfut, Claudine, editors. *Educational and Leisure Time Activities of the Elderly*. Prague: European Centre for Leisure and Education, 1973.

2. Coleman, James. *American Psychological Association Monitor*, February 1973.

3. *Annotated Bibliography on Leisure: Poland (1960–1970)*. Bibliographic Series No. 3. Prague: European Centre for Leisure and Education, 1971.

4. Foreign Trade Agency. *Polish Economy Survey*. Warsawa, 1974, II (296), p. 7. Polish Interpress Agency. *Panorama of Polish Industry, 1944–1974*.

5. Rokkan, Stein. "Cross-Cultural, Cross-Societal and Cross-National Research." *Main Trends of Research in the Social and Human Sciences*. Paris, The Hague: UNESCO, Mouton, 1970. Chapter X.

6. Szydlak, Jan. Speech to national conference, Warsaw, January 8, 1973.

7. Wnuk'-Lipinski, Edmund. "Job Satisfaction and the Quality of Working Life: The Polish Experience." *International Labour Review* 115; January–February 1977.

8. Dumazedier, Joffre, *op. cit.*, pp. 169–173.

9. *Cultural Affairs* 1: 1–2. Bulletin of the Department of Cultural Research and Planning, Ministry of Culture and Art, Baharesten, Tehran, Iran. October 1974.

10. Dumazedier, Joffre, *op. cit.*, p. 166.

11. Richta, Radovan, editor, *op. cit.*

12. Bell, Daniel. *The Coming of Post-Industrial Society, op. cit.*